From Our
Mothers'
Arms

The Intergenerational Impact of Residential Schools in Saskatchewan

Constance Deiter

UNITED CHURCH PUBLISHING HOUSE
Toronto, Ontario

From Our Mothers' Arms
The Intergenerational Impact of Residential Schools in Saskatchewan

All biblical quotations, unless otherwise noted, are from the *New Revised Standard Version Bible*, copyright © 1989, by the Division of Christian Education of the National Council of the Churches of Christ in the United States of America. Used by permission.

Canadian Cataloguing in Publication Data

Deiter, Constance, 1953-
    From our mothers' arms : the intergenerational impact of residential schools in Saskatchewan

Includes bibliographical references.
ISBN 1-55134-095-X

1. Native peoples - Saskatchewan - Residential schools.* 2. Native peoples - Education - Saskatchewan.* 3. Native peoples - Cultural assimilation - Saskatchewan.* I. Title

E96.65.S3D44 1998   371.829'707124   C98-932691-8

United Church Publishing House
3250 Bloor Street West, Suite 300
Etobicoke ON
Canada M8X 2Y4
416-231-5931
bookpub@uccan.org

Design, Editorial, and Production: Department of Publishing and Graphics

Printed in Canada
5 4 3 2   03 02 01

980376

Contents

To Walter and Inez Deiter
and my sons Matthew and Jonathan

Foreword

It is my pleasure to provide a short foreword to this book that, I believe, is a valuable addition to the growing body of written material examining the history and impact of residential schools on Aboriginal peoples across Canada.

In particular, I like the fact that Ms. Deiter anchored her book on the personal reminiscences of people from her own family and community. It is their words, their stories, that breathe life into the dry facts and figures often used to illuminate this unhappy period in Canada's history. As we might expect, they had many different experiences and they speak to us now with different voices. As they tell their all-too human stories, they convey the wide range of emotions their experiences gave them, from the puzzlement, the bitterness, the hurt, and the anger we have come to expect, right through to the laughter that still catches me by surprise. Not all the stories are about abuse, and their inclusion adds some important balance to the discussion. In fact, there is humour in some of these stories, and it stands as a testament to the strength of those who survived such a prolonged assault on their personal and collective sense of Aboriginal self-esteem.

Ms. Deiter's book does something else as well: by collecting interviews primarily from the senior members of her own extended family, she gives us a very immediate sense of how the residential school experience touched not just individuals but whole communities. As the stories unfold, it becomes clear that it was not a case of isolated individuals sustaining losses and then returning to a healthy social context, but of almost everyone sustaining virtually identical losses—and having only an unhealthy, strategically disrupted social context to return to. It was that wholesale disruption that spawned the degree of family and community breakdown that now plagues so many Aboriginal communities, and Ms. Dieter's transcripts take us, emotionally and intellectually, back to the period when it all began.

Finally, I like the way Ms. Deiter's commentary identified and highlighted the various strands woven within the personal stories she collected. With her help, we can see the many themes emerging, moving past the more blatant forms of abuse to see for ourselves how school practices made it almost impossible for boys and girls to learn what it meant to become respectful spouses to each other or parents to their children.

I congratulate Ms. Deiter for her work. I congratulate her interviewees for the courage they showed by speaking in such a public way. And I congratulate The United Church of Canada for supporting this project through to publication. The restoration of health to Aboriginal Canada requires brave voices and strong hearts, and everyone associated with *From Our Mothers' Arms* has helped to show the way.

Rupert Ross

Preface

Long before my people journeyed to this land, your people
were here, and you received from your elders understanding of creation and mystery that surrounds us all, that was
deep and to be treasured. We did not hear you when you
shared your vision. In our zeal to tell you the good news of
Jesus Christ we were closed to the values of your spirituality. We confused western ways and culture ways, the depth
and breadth and length and height of the gospel of Christ.
We imposed our civilization as a condition of accepting
the gospel. We tried to make you like us and in doing so we
helped destroy the vision that made you what you were. As
a result you and we are poorer. And the image of the creator in us is twisted and blurred and we are not what we
are meant by to be. We ask you to forgive us and to walk
together with us in the spirit of Christ so that our people
may be blessed and God's creation healed.

Robert S. Smith,
Moderator of The United Church of Canada, Sudbury, 1986[1]

In the spirit of the apology of 1986, The United Church of Canada
has made a commitment to assist First Nations individuals and communities to heal from the experiences of the Indian residential
schools. The commitment takes the form of a healing fund called
"The United Church Healing Fund in Response to the Hurt of Native Residential Schools." Money is raised through voluntary
contributions from individuals in the church community and the
general public. The goal for the fund is to reach $1 million dollars
within five years (1995 to 1999). Individuals and First Nations communities will then be able to access the fund for projects that will
assist in the healing process.

As part of the entire United Church's commitment, the
Saskatchewan Conference established the Residential School Listening Panel. The panel, established in 1993, was to investigate the
circumstances of the residential schools in Saskatchewan in which

the United Church participated. Panel members included Reverend Bill Wall, Sharon Davis, Janet Sigurdson, and Richard Hazel. After several meetings with former students of the schools, the panel decided that their stories should be told to the general membership. The stories you are about to read were compiled to create greater awareness of the legacy of the residential schools in our communities. Other churches also participated in residential schools in Saskatchewan; however, for this publication most of the interviews were recorded from students who attended United Church residential schools.

From Our Mothers' Arms was initiated to create more awareness of the effects residential schools had on First Nations communities. It is hoped that, as the general membership becomes more knowledgeable, church members will acknowledge and demonstrate the spirit of the 1986 apology through direct action. That action could be in the form of contributions to the Healing Fund. Marion Best, past moderator of The United Church of Canada, has said "I believe The Healing Fund will result in increased understanding and commitment by United Church people to address the many injustices that have been perpetrated against First Nations people over the centuries."[2]

Finally, Reverend Stan McKay, a former student of the Brandon Indian Residential school, and another recent moderator of The United Church of Canada wrote:

> The removal of children (to residential schools) from the family hastened the impact of cultural genocide. I experienced five years in an Indian residential school. It was a period of incarceration that affected my self-confidence and my self-worth in negative ways. I am marked by the experience of the suffering of young children without adequate care and physical abuse of elder children who could not conform. The Healing Fund will be a beacon of hope for those seeking to free themselves from this historic oppression. It will enable people to gather in circles of healing, and there will be an empowering of many for healing.[3]

The Healing Fund in Response to the Hurt of Native Residential Schools can be accessed by any community or individual who may need funding to pursue a healing initiative within a First Nations community. Inquiries as to fund applications or contributions can be made directly to:

The Healing Fund
The United Church of Canada
Suite 300, 3250 Bloor Street West
Etobicoke, ON M8X 2Y4
416-231-5931 ext. 5047
fax 416-232-6005

SOUTHEASTERN SASKATCHEWAN

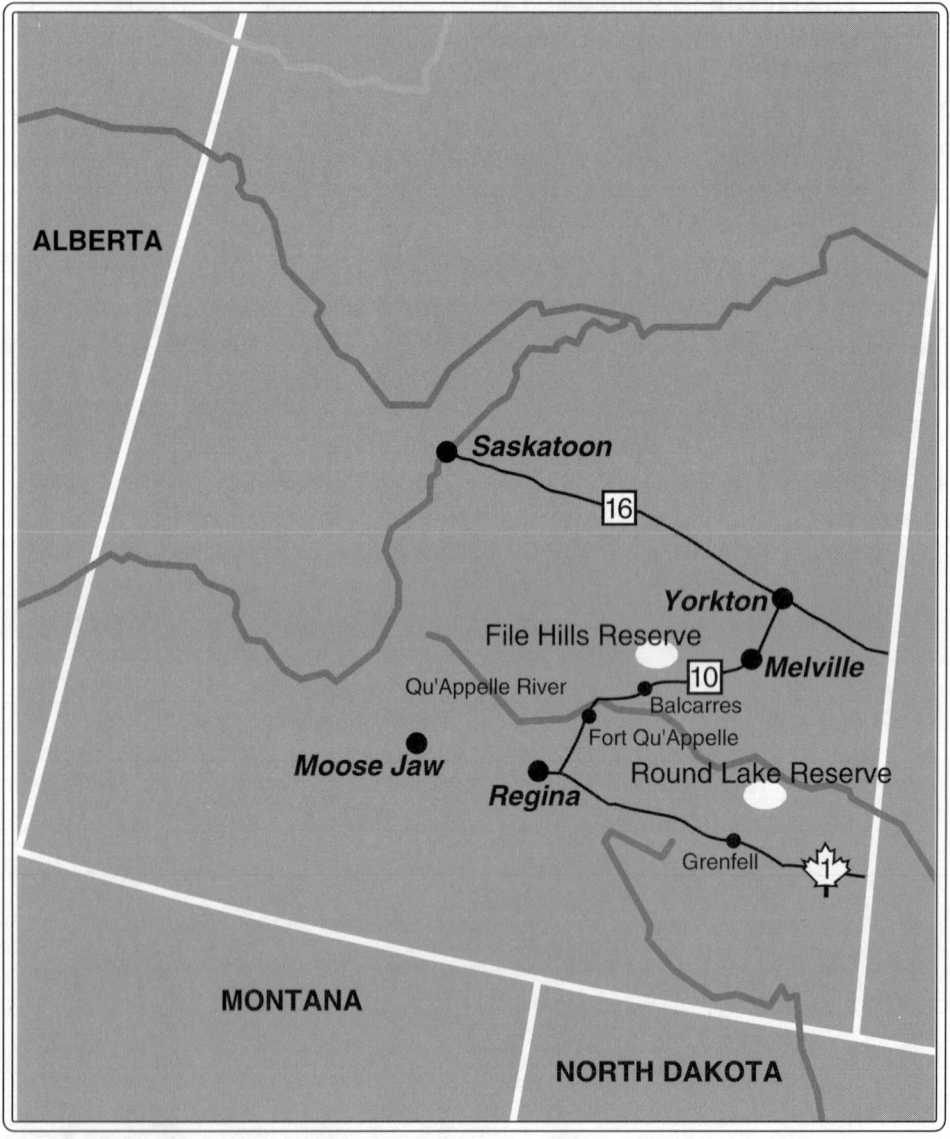

ALBERTA

Saskatoon

16

Yorkton

File Hills Reserve

Qu'Appelle River

10

Melville

Balcarres

Fort Qu'Appelle

Moose Jaw

Round Lake Reserve

Regina

Grenfell

1

MONTANA

NORTH DAKOTA

Map not to scale.

Acknowledgements

I am extremely grateful for my mother Inez Deiter's assistance with this book, as well as my sister Pat Deiter who directed me to interviews housed at the Saskatchewan Indian Federated College. I thank the Glenbow Foundation for allowing me to use a chapter from *I Walk in Two Worlds* written by my aunt, Eleanor Brass; the Listening Panel of Saskatchewan Conference; and Janet Deiter Sigurdson.

Of course, my deepest gratitude goes to the women and men who shared their stories for this book. Their courage and generosity of spirit are steps towards healing in our community.

Part I

Preparing for the Interviews

Part 1

Establishing the Interview

1
Background

It is only within the past thirty years that any serious research has been done to examine the Indian residential school experience. Previous research was directed at the systemics of teaching Indian children, but not at the experiences of the children themselves. In fact, the earliest comprehensive report on Indian education in Canada was not completed until 1966, and even then, the study did not discuss the living conditions of the children.

In 1966, the Hawthorn report, titled *A Survey of Contemporary Indians of Canada*,[1] was commissioned by the federal government after the 1951 changes to the Indian Act.[2] It came about because the government realized they knew little about Indian people and, in particular, the circumstances and social dynamics of Indian education. For this report a group of anthropologists and educators researched and interviewed administrators and First Nations officials to determine the state of education in Indian country. They found a dismal record of inadequate facilities, substandard curriculum, and too few teaching aides and teachers. The report led to the movement towards integrating the residential schools with the provincial government-run school systems. For most advocates, this meant a higher standard of education for Indian children. Curiously, although the report covered the existing residential schools, it focused on facilities, curriculum, and teaching standards, but not on the living conditions of the children attending the schools.

There were several reasons for this lack of attention. The primary reason was that the researchers looked at education from a middle-class, non-Aboriginal perspective. They determined that the purpose of the study of education was just that—education. They did not understand that Indian education was inherently different because of the residential school experience. The study should have included the living environment of the Indian children.

However, even if the research mandate were expanded to include the living circumstances of Indian children while attending school, it would have been unlikely that research would have found a high incidence of abuse, because of the reluctance of Indian students to speak freely of their experiences. At the time of the Hawthorn report, public disclosure of abuses of any kind was still many years away, and most Indian residential school survivors were still in denial, unwilling or unable to face, or even recognize, the abuse they had suffered. Even when I was compiling stories for this book, recalcitrance was still an issue among former students.

Another reason for the likely failure to uncover stories of abuse was that Indian political activism was in its infancy. In the early 1960s, Indian people, for the most part, had no voice. Indian organizations were beginning, but lacked the political influence they would later gain. Our voices were silenced.

The continued existence of the Indian residential schools well into the 1960s was another factor in the Hawthorn report's failure to examine students' living conditions. In 1969 Saskatchewan still had six residential schools in operation. Across Canada, the Department of Indian Affairs was operating 62 schools. Some 9,000 Indian students were still attending those schools, despite the Department of Indian Affairs and the churches' attempts to move away from the residential school model.[3]

Yet Indian Affairs found the schools too costly to operate, and the schools were becoming troublesome to officials. Stories of abuse were beginning to make their way to the head offices of both the churches and the schools, and questions were being raised as to the liability of those involved in the administration of the institutions. In addition, there was a change taking place across Indian country and in the schools themselves. Indian students were being influenced by the general social unrest in the United states and Canada. At the Edmonton Indian Residential School operated jointly by the United Church and the federal government, for example, a riot took place among the students in 1962 as students expressed their displeasure at their living conditions and treatment.[4]

Whatever the reasons, the residential school aspects of Indian education were not adequately researched by academics, clergy, or government until very recently. Furthermore, the little research that was done was conducted from a non–First Nations viewpoint. This book is an attempt to present a picture of the residential school experience from the eyes and memories of First Nations' people. It will illustrate that the residential school experience for most First Nations individuals is an intergenerational experience, one that didn't stop with one student, but affected every generation and each of us in the Indian community at a profound and personal level.

To provide some background, clarification of the terms used to describe Aboriginal people is necessary. The Aboriginal people of Canada refer to the Métis, Status or non-Status Indians, and Inuit. The Métis are the descendants of a Status Indian and a European and have been recognized as a separate people since before Confederation. Status Indians are the descendants of Indians who signed the eleven numbered treaties with the federal government and are registered under the Indian Act. Non-Status Indians are those Aboriginal people who were recognized as Indians by the federal government but lost their status through marriage or other provisions under the Indian Act.

Another category is non-Treaty Indians, people whose ancestors never signed a treaty, but received Indian status. Since the 1985 changes to the Indian Act, which allowed non-Status Indians to regain their status, they have been considered First Nations people, or Indians. Inuit are descendants of the people who were called "Eskimo" until the late 1970s, when they asserted their right to be called Inuit, which in their language means "people." Eskimo is a Cree word that was thought to be derogatory because it means "fish eaters."

The Indian residential school experience affected only Status Indians, non-Treaty Indians, and Inuit. In a few cases, Métis children were allowed to attend the schools. There are several archival references made by local priests or agents who allowed a Métis child to attend school, but these occurrences were rare. It should be made clear that the effects of the Indian residential school system are found only in the Indian and Inuit communities of Canada. The Métis did not have restrictions placed on them by the Indian Act and were not affected by the residential school experience.

RECENT PUBLICATIONS

Since the 1980s, authors like Brian Titley, Cecelia Haig-Brown, Linda Jaine, and J. R. Miller have published research on the Indian residential schools. Brian Titley's book, *A Narrow Vision*, published in 1986, was one of the first to look at Indian education in Canada. Although he wrote only one chapter on the residential school experience, he did mention a few recorded cases of abuse found in the Department of Indian Affairs records. But overall, the book focused on the administrative relationship between Indian people and department officials.[5]

By the time Cecelia Haig-Brown's book, *Resistance and Renewal*[6] was released in 1988, it was a type of vindication. The book included interviews with former students that were frank testimonials of the sexual, physical, and emotional abuse of students at the Catholic-run Kamloops Indian Residential School in British Columbia. Although her interviews were restricted to the Kamloops students, their stories sounded very much like those that were coming out of just about any residential school in Canada. Haig-Brown's book was a breakthrough for survivors. Finally, people were beginning to tell outsiders stories of the abuse that Indian people experienced as commonplace. Unfortunately, the book did not receive the attention it

Thomas Moore before and after attending the Regina Industrial School, n.d.

deserved, probably because people were not yet ready to accept the truth of the stories of abuse.

Although not the first account written by First Nations authors, the 1994 report of the Assembly of First Nations, *Breaking the Silence*,[7] seems to have done just that: it broke the silence. The report sanctioned the right of other survivors to speak about their personal stories of neglect and abuse. Shortly afterwards, former students began to file claims in court against their abusers. British Columbia survivors were the first to begin actions against a church and the individuals who ran the schools. Bishop O'Connor's case was the first to be made public. His first trial and the subsequent media coverage portrayed him as a man unduly accused, but the British Columbia Court of Appeal confirmed what many in Indian country knew to be true: he was a man who abused children, despite his religious collar or his standing.[8]

Two First Nations authors, Linda Bull and Linda Jaine, also published accounts of recorded interviews with former students. Linda Bull investigated the experiences of students who attended schools in Northern Alberta. The result of her investigations was the publication of part of her Master's thesis as "Indian Residential Schools: The Native Perspective."[9] Linda Jaine's book, *Residential Schools: The Stolen Years*,[10] compiled interviews with students who attended schools in central Saskatchewan. Linda Jaine was also involved in hosting a gathering of survivors of the schools. A video with the same name was produced; it is available through the Saskatchewan Indian Federated College.

The most recent, and probably the most well received book, was written by J. R. Miller, a professor of history at the University of Saskatchewan. His book, *Shingwauk's Vision*,[11] is well researched and documented. However, I have some concerns over his interpretation of some of his research findings. For example, included in the back of the book is a photograph of the Lebret Indian Industrial school with teepees and carts set up outside the schoolyard. Miller sees this as evidence that school administrators allowed parents to visit.

My grandfather, Fred Dieter,* told me a different story about those teepees outside the schools. He remembered, as a young child, teepees camped outside the school grounds for months. They housed the parents and grandparents of the children living at the school. He understood that the parents camped outside the school

---

*Walter Deiter, my father, changed the spelling of the family name.

in hopes of catching a glimpse of their children. In the photograph there is a scraped hide frame and several carts, teepees, and tents. Since the practice of Indian people is to construct temporary structures if they intended to stay for only a few days, the people in the photographs, with their hide-frame teepees, carts, and tents, look as if they intended to stay for a much longer time. I commend Professor Miller for the massive research for his book, but the real stories about residential schools can only be told by Indian people themselves.

CALLS FOR AN INQUIRY

In the early 1990s several calls for an inquiry into the schools were raised by former students. One of the first public figures to call for an inquiry was Phil Fontaine, then the head of the Manitoba Chiefs Federation. He went public with his own story of physical and sexual abuse, which took place at the Catholic-run Fort Alexander Indian Residential School in Manitoba. In a letter to the editor of *The Globe and Mail* he said, "I think what happened to me is what happened to a lot of people. It wasn't just sexual abuse, it was physical and psychological abuse. It was a violation."[12]

Mel H. Buffalo, spokesperson for the Indian Association of Alberta, and a former residential school student, also wrote to *The Globe and Mail*, claiming that, "Everyone that I have spoken to who has attended the schools has a story of physical, sexual or emotional abuse."[13] He also called for a national inquiry into the Indian residential school experience to investigate what he called the "legacy of chaos" that these schools left in our communities. First Nations leaders across the country demanded a full-scale investigation to examine the role the churches and government played in Indian residential schools.

Chief Blaine Favel, former chief of the Federation of Saskatchewan Indians, was critical of the Department of Indian Affairs' handling of the abuses at the Gordon Indian Residential School operated by the Anglican church and the federal government in Punnichy, Saskatchewan. This school was under scrutiny because its administrator from the 1960s to the 1980s, William Peniston Starr, was charged (and convicted in 1993), with numerous counts of sexual assault against several young boys who attended the school.[14] Without admitting any wrongdoing, the Department of Indian Affairs agreed to provide financial compensation to the victims.

Nevertheless, there was a court-ordered publication ban on the amount paid to the victims by the Department of Indian Affairs.

Despite these calls for an inquiry, then Minister of Indian Affairs Tom Siddon was adamant: there would be no inquiry into the Indian residential school experience. His reaction may have been because of another orphanage inquiry that sent shock waves across the country: the Mount Cashel inquiry and subsequent trials of Christian Brothers in Newfoundland.[15] Because of the shocking nature of the Mount Cashel victims' stories, many people believed that the Department of Indian Affairs would not risk public scrutiny of the stories of the abuses that took place at Indian residential schools over an eighty-year span.

Then, in 1991, the government reversed its position and established the Royal Commission on Aboriginal Peoples with a mandate to investigate government policy regarding the Aboriginal peoples of this country, particularly with regard to Indian land claims.[16] Critics argued that the commission was set up to bury the call for an inquiry into the Indian residential schools. The five-volume report devoted only sixty pages to the abuses suffered by residential school students.

PREPARING FOR THE INTERVIEWS

As a First Nations person, I believed I understood the effects that Indian residential schools had upon our communities. Certainly as a student of First Nations studies I had read most of the literature written about the residential school experience and knew many of the stories were filled with pain. Still, I distanced myself from those stories because they were about other schools and happened to other people. When I agreed to gather interviews for the Listening Panel of the Saskatchewan Conference of The United Church of Canada, I thought this objectivity would carry me through the project. Not so. After I began researching my own community, it became apparent that I really did not understand the collective effects the schools had had on my community, my family, and myself.

This book records interviews that were collected from individuals in my community. I want to emphasize that many of the interviews requested were not completed. For many of the survivors, the experiences of the schools were too difficult to recall.

Many of the interviews and stories are from family members and from people from my childhood. Throughout the book there is an intentional shift in voice because I have interwoven material gathered from the historical records with information gathered through the oral history of my family. The result is a journey to understanding the effects Indian residential schools had and continue to have on the lives of Indian people of Saskatchewan.

At the onset of the interviews, I expected strong support from members of my community for the project. Indeed, at local community meetings held with the Listening Panel of the Saskatchewan Conference of the United Church, community members were vocal about the abuses that happened at the File Hills Indian Residential School. However, the anticipated support for the project was not the reality. For example, while preparing for the interviews, I would call the night before to confirm the interviewee's participation but, on more than one occasion, the interviewee was not available. After several attempts with different survivors, I realized the implications of these "no-shows." They were a non-confrontational Indian way of telling me they were not going to give an interview. In one situation, I received a call from a family member who confided in the me that after one initial interview session, the man I had interviewed had left the house and got drunk. The caller said that I was welcome to visit, but I could no longer question about the residential school experience. I can only speculate about the pain this person endured while attending the school. The man was over seventy years old and was an individual I knew through my childhood. He attended the same school as my father and at the same time period. These were the adults who had surrounded me in childhood.

Eventually I did manage to record interviews with former students of residential schools situated in Saskatchewan and Manitoba. The ages of the participants range from early fifties to over seventy years of age. They are all from a Plains tribal group, but most are Plains Cree. John Haywaha is from the Nakota nation. All the participants attended schools run by The United Church of Canada, except for Inez Deiter, who attended a Roman Catholic school and an Anglican school.

The protocol for the interviews included the First Nations practice of exchanging tobacco and cloth for the information I was to receive. Most of the interviews were conducted in the participants' homes. Conversation was shared over a cup of tea. For some interviews I would bring my mother Inez Deiter to translate and put the participant at ease.

2

An Intergenerational Experience

The most terrible result of my residential school experience was they took away my ability to hold my children. They took that from me, the ability to hold my children.

—my mother, Inez Deiter

For the majority of First Nations people living in Canada, the Indian residential school experience is an intergenerational experience that extends through four or five generations. For my family, the residential school experience began in the late 1800s, with my paternal grandfather and grandmother. Fred Dieter and Marybelle Dieter (Côté) both attended the Regina Industrial School in the late 1890s. This chapter follows my paternal grandfather's experience with the schools as I have more information about his experience than my maternal grandfather's. Fred Dieter distinguished himself at the school and later as a farmer in the File Hills Colony on the Peepeekisis Reserve in southern Saskatchewan. There is a fair amount of research written about him. I spent many summers with him on his farm listening to his stories.

BACKGROUND TO THE SCHOOLS
Residential schools for Indian people have been established tradition since at least the sixteenth century. They have a long history, which probably began with the Montagnais and the Algonkian-speaking

tribes of eastern Canada. The Franciscans were the first to establish a residential school, in 1620.[1] After the Franciscans fell out of favour with the French government, the Jesuits took over the official task of mission work. The Jesuits soon adopted the residential school plan for Indian students.

The Jesuits were the first to suggest the problems of assimilating Indian children while the children still lived with their families. The Jesuits actively recruited children to their missions and took advantage of Algonkian practices and beliefs to do so. The Algonkians had the practice of sharing their children with those who did not have children.[2] The Algonkians also practised intertribal adoption with warring neighbours. The idea behind this practice is that the enemy (or your own people) would reconsider attacking a village if children from their own village were living in an enemy camp. Both practices ensured alliances and peaceful co-existence between either two warring tribal groups or between two nations.

The Jesuits continued with the residential school experiments for a few more years, but the lack of converts among the Indian people, coupled with the refusal of many Indian parents to have their children taken from them, soon closed many of the schools.

It is noteworthy that the Jesuits suggested four major changes necessary to civilize Indian people. These included introducing a central autocratic form of governance. They wrote that Indians

Fred Dieter in the soccer team at the Regina Industrial School, standing second from right, 1894 or 5

"imagine that they ought by right of birth, to enjoy the liberty of wild ass colts, rendering no homage to anyone whomsoever, except when they like."[3] They also wanted to change the role of women to a more European model, with an authoritarian male and subservient female, and to outlaw divorce. They thought Indian women had too high a standing in Indian society. As well, they wanted to introduce the concept of punishment into Algonkian society, especially for children, and to have children taught in the missions away from their parents and community.[4]

Later, the residential school model was expanded to include non-Indians. In the mid-eighteenth century industrial schools were established in eastern Canada for destitute women and children as an alternative to the poorhouses or workhouses found in Europe.[5] The "inmates," as they were called, would work for their upkeep. At some schools, Indian children and non-Indian children were placed together. The administrators of the school thought that the presence of European children would assimilate the Indian children at a greater speed.

Unfortunately for Indian people, the residential school model would not fade away, but it would be picked up as quickly as others would discard it. Since the first school opened in the 1600s there have been Indian children living in a residential school environment for the last three hundred years.

In western Canada, the experience came at a later period, but because of a stronger central government, its effects were more strongly felt. In 1810 religious denominations were operating day schools in western Canada along the fur trade route. Reports from missionaries stated that they were having the same difficulties as their predecessors in eastern Canada. Indian children were not attending school on a regular basis. To keep the schools open, non-Indian children were included in many day schools operated by religious denominations. At this time, it was not compulsory for Indian children to attend schools. Missionaries would use food rations to entice Indian parents to place their children in the schools. The practice began with the Jesuits but was continued well into the nineteenth century.

GOVERNMENT POLICY

Indian residential schools were established because of the historical relationship between Canadian Indians and the British Crown. After Confederation, this historical relationship was entrenched in the Constitution under section 91(24) of the British North America Act. This followed from previous policy wherein the British government made alliances with the Indian nations during the French and American wars. Unfortunately, this relationship changed as Europeans settlement in eastern Canada increased. After Confederation, Indians were still seen as wards of the British Crown, but they were wards who had some legal association to the land that was to become Canada.[6]

As a result of its mandate under the Constitution to deal with Indians, the government began a process for extinguishing the legal association by a series of treaties. Chief Okanese, Fred Dieter's grandfather, was to sign Treaty Number Four on behalf of his band in 1874.

Treaties between the First Nations and European governments were established practice prior to the treaties signed in western Canada. The British government, through its Royal Proclamation of 1763, acknowledged an aboriginal right to the land by First Nations inhabitants. This proclamation established a process for extinguishing this right, one that would only allow First Nations people to relinquish this right to the Crown. The new Canadian government wanted to open up the western territories for settlement, and began to negotiate treaties with First Nations in parts of the country.

Prior to the western treaties, the official Canadian policy was to protect, civilize, and assimilate the Indian.[7] The Gradual Civilization Act, passed in 1857, called for the eventual assimilation of Indians into Canadian society. It was later consolidated with other acts dealing with Indians and Indian lands into the Indian Act, 1876. This Act was actually in force before the treaties in the west were signed, but it was never mentioned to the Indians during treaty negotiations. The Indians were led to believe they could continue their traditional way of life, and that the provisions made by treaty would merely add to what they already had.

For the Indians of the West, this seemed a fair exchange. They knew their way of life was changing, and that, to survive, they had to learn a new lifestyle. This is one of the reasons chiefs asked for schools to be built on their reserves. At first, the government made attempts to pay for these day schools, as they were called, but the schools were not a priority. In order to reduce costs, the government contracted with the churches to supply teachers to these new schools. This plan set in motion the relationships among the churches, the federal government, and the Indians that led to the residential school model. The churches were to supply the administrators and teachers while the government supplied the costs for any capital and ongoing expenses. The day schools turned out to be unsuccessful for the church and the government, primarily because of the irregular attendance by the Indian students and the difficulty in finding teachers. Another concern for government was that even when the children did attend regularly, students would return to the influence of their parents and their Indian ways. The department needed to find other methods of assimilation.

In 1879 Nicholas Davin, a lawyer-journalist, prepared a report on the Indian residential school system operating in the United States. His report was enthusiastically accepted by Sir John A. MacDonald. This report called for compulsory education for all Indian children and also recommended contracting with the churches to administer the schools. The first step towards the Indian residential school system was introduced through amendments to the Indian Act. The new policy included compulsory education for Indian children between the ages of six and sixteen. The policy had changed from the previous one in that it severed the children's link to their ancestral homes and ensured they were educated in European lifestyle and values.

The Roman Catholic, Anglican, Methodist, and Presbyterian churches welcomed the opportunity to broaden their flock. For years, the missionaries had been asking the department to introduce compulsory education in a residential school environment. Between the church and state, there was a combined effort to undermine traditional Indian beliefs.

The first residential schools were called industrial schools. These were modeled after the Carlisle School in Pennsylvania. Students were provided with minimal educational skills, but their education was supplemented with instruction in trades, farming, and animal husbandry. The Regina Industrial School was one of the first such schools established in Canada. In operation between 1895 and 1910, it had a printing shop, a blacksmithing shop, and a carpentry shop. It also provided the basic literacy and numeracy skills.

Industrial schools had a short existence because of the unexpected costs and a change in immigration patterns. Frank Oliver, a notable Member of Parliament, wrote that "we are educating Indians to compete industrially with our own people, which seems to me a very undesirable use of public money."[8] Criticisms like these resulted in changes to the curriculum in the residential school model.

Indeed, a 1904 Indian Department memo stated, "It was never the policy of the department, nor the design of the industrial school to turn out Indian pupils to compete with the whites."[9] Thus, the new schools were to produce farmers and housekeepers, not employees and servants. The curriculum still included basic literacy skills and agricultural skills for farming. The boys were taught farming techniques and animal husbandry while the girls were taught the tasks of running a household. Attendance was compulsory for all Indian students. Survivors and written testimony state that any runaways were to be brought back under police escort, and parents who refused to send their children were subject to a fine or imprisonment for six months or withholding of rations. Whether or not these provisions were actually followed across the country, the point is that Indian people believed they were in force. Furthermore, in my interviews, stories of runaways brought back under police escort were common.

The first residential school administered by the Presbyterians in Saskatchewan was at Round Lake near Broadview, which was established 1886. Most students were from the Crooked Lake bands, which includes the Ochapowace, Kakawistahow, Cowessess, and Sakimay.

The File Hills Residential School was located on the Okanese reserve north of Balcarres, Saskatchewan. The school opened in 1889 and closed in 1949. The school was surrounded by the reserves of the File Hills agency, including Peepeekisis, Okanese, Little Black Bear, and Starblanket. My family and members of the File Hills community attended this school. Most of the Presbyterian Indian students from Saskatchewan attended these schools; others attended the Brandon and Birtle schools in Manitoba. The general understanding was that Brandon was the only school in which Presbyterian and Methodist Indian students could receive a high school education. A student would first attend the File Hills or Round Lake school and then would move to Brandon to enter high school. My father and uncles followed this pattern.

My grandfather Fred Dieter would later become one of the most successful farmers in southern Saskatchewan. He was one of the first farmers, Indian or white, to own an automobile in the Balcarres re-

Fred Dieter, left, and his barn, horses, and non-Native hired man, 1915

gion. The fact that he hired white workers on his farm is mentioned several times in departmental records and later in books. However, despite his wealth and standing, he was still an Indian and was forced to send his children to residential school. Eleanor Brass recalls that her father purchased land off the reserve and paid the taxes. He did this so that his children could attend the white school in the town of Lorlie. However, the Indian agent took his children out of the school and sent them back to residential school.

LITTLE KITCHI-MOOKHO-MAN

This is where my family story begins. My grandfather, or *Moosum*, was Fred Dieter and he was born in 1880. He was the grandson of Chief Okanese, signator for Treaty Four. Chief Okanese was the son of "the Fox," a major Cree chief in the early 1800s. A picture of the Fox can be found in Henry Hind's narratives.[10] Hind wrote that the Fox was highly regarded for his skills as a hunter, trader, linguist, scout, and warrior. The Fox was the son of Legion of Many Eagles, another major chief in the prairie region. Edward Ahenakew wrote that Legion of Many Eagles would send his sons to establish trading partners among the tribes of what are now known as Manitoba and Saskatchewan. Another son, Le Sonnet, signed the Selkirk Treaty in Manitoba in 1817.[11] The Fox had two sons who later also become chiefs: Okanese and Pasqua.

Treaty pay lists and family history state that Fred's mother was the daughter of Chief Okanese. Her marriage to an American buffalo hunter named Charlie Dieter was arranged by her father. The Indians called him "Kitchi-mookho-man." This word translates from Cree as Long Knife or Long Knife man. It identifies him as possibly American. He might have been with the American Calvary at some time and possibly wore a uniform with a sword—hence the name Long Knife. My aunt writes that Kitchi-mookho-man was a respected friend of the chief. Kitchi-mookho-man and my great-grandmother were married by Father Hugonnard in Lebret, Saskatchewan.

The relationship did not last long. My great-grandmother missed her Indian people and their ways, so she left her husband and returned to her father's camp. Little Kitchi-mookho-man was born at Okanese's village. He was loved very much by his mother's family, but the family worried that Charlie Dieter would someday come and take his son away, especially when there were stories about a rebellion in the north (the Riel uprising). Okanese sent his grandson away with others from his band to the Dakota hills during the rebellion to ensure their safety. The senior Kitchi-mookho-man did return to the Indian village to retrieve his son, but was told his son had died. When the rebellion was over, the Indians brought Little Kitchi-mookho-man back to their traditional camping grounds.

A *Regina Leader* account described a treaty negotiation trip made by Edgar Dewdney, the Commissioner of Indian Affairs, and his aides.[12] One of the scouts who travelled with this group to Blackfoot territory was an old buffalo hunter named Charlie Dieter. The article told about a wiry American buffalo hunter who lived with the File Hills Cree. Charlie Dieter left Canada for the United States shortly after the Riel troubles in the north started. He never returned but a lake and a road are named after him in the File Hills area, north of Balcarres, Saskatchewan. Fred's mother died in an epidemic after the ride to the United States during the Riel uprising. Little Kitchi-mookho-man was raised by his *moosum*, Chief Okanese. Treaty pay lists for this period record Chief Okanese, "Red Stone Woman" (my great-great-grandmother), and a grandson living as a family unit since 1883. The payments were transferred to the Regina Industrial School in 1894.

In European society, Little Kitchi-mookho-man would have been an orphan, but in the Indian world there is no such thing. Orphans or adopted children were not treated any differently by the band; in fact, they were cherished as were all children of the band. For Little Kitchi-mookho-man, this was particularly true. Family lore adds to the story of the trip to the Dakotas during the uprising. The chief was very concerned that Charlie Dieter would encounter the group. He told his warriors that if Charlie Dieter attempted to take his son, they were to murder him. This would ensure his grandson would be brought back to his village.

During one of the summers I spent with my grandfather he told about the ride to the United States during the uprising. He said he remembered riding on the back of a dog and travelling at night so as to not encounter any soldiers. As a young person, I never really believed this story but later, as a university student, I went to a museum and saw dog saddles.

Little Kitchi-mookho-man lived a traditional childhood. Childhood for all Indian children was a time of great indulgence and freedom. This First Nations attitude caused much concern for the European missionaries. One of the first to lament about this was the Jesuit priest Le Jeune. He argued that the children should be taken and placed in schools, "because these barbarians can not bear to have their children punished, even scolded, not being able to refuse anything to a crying child."[13] Two centuries later, David Mandelbaum, a noted ethnologist of the Plains Cree, supports this idea that Indian children were never corporally punished. "They were never beaten and rarely reprimanded...even during the most sacred rights children were accorded perfect liberty."[14]

Traditional Plains tribal education for children involved imitating adults and experimental teachings. My aunt wrote that Little Kitchi-mookho-man learned how to hunt and trap like his tribesmen. When he killed his first rabbit, there was a traditional feast and he was honoured for his accomplishment. Young girls were given dolls to care for and were also responsible for the care of younger children. These practices were based on love and respect. Plains Cree believe that children are only on loan and are a gift of the Creator. Within this belief, children are not regarded as possessions.

When Little Kitchi-mookho-man returned to his Moosum's camps, he also found missionaries living near the village. One of the first Presbyterian mission day schools in western Canada was built on the Okanese reserve.

Another story my grandfather told was of the time when the first missionaries moved in among them. He told us that he had an uncle named Pimotat who would sell Little Kitchi-mookho-man to the highest bidder or missionary for a bag of flour. This was before the 1894 Canadian law that forced Indian children to attend school. The plan was for Little Kitchi-mookho-man to go with the missionaries and stay a few days, then run home. My grandfather said Chief Okanese's people received many bags of flour. It did not matter which denomination he ran away from. He attended both the Roman Catholic school and the Presbyterian school.

One day he could not run away, and was forced to stay at the latest school. In 1894, changes were made to the Indian Act that made attendance at residential school compulsory for all able-bodied Indian children. Under the provisions of this Act, officials were allowed to take any course of action to ensure attendance. For Little Kitchi-mookho-man, it was the last time he would live with his beloved *moosum*, Chief Okanese. This was the same year that treaty money paid previously to Red Stone Woman for her grandson, Fred Dieter, was transferred to the Regina Industrial School.

My grandfather's memories of his first day of residential school were of losing his braids and wearing white man's clothes. My aunt would later write that Little Kitchi-mookho-man felt very sad for his lovely hair. It must have been traumatic for him because, in his story to me, he repeated his sorrow at the loss of his braids.

Previously, I mentioned the picture of the teepees camped outside the school. I wonder if my grandfather saw similar teepees. On those summer evenings spent on the porch he told me that as a young man he would see teepees camped outside the school for months. They were the teepees of the parents and families of the children who were taken away and living at the school. They camped outside in hopes of catching a glimpse of their children. Perhaps, old Chief Okanese was one of those camped outside the schoolyard.

The Department of Indian Affairs policy was to have Indian children removed from the influences of their parents and community. The policy took into account that although they were educating

Indian children in the ways of the European, there was a risk that they might fall back to the ways of their parents, if contact was encouraged at the schools. Both J. R. Miller and Eleanor Brass in their books mention the practice of keeping the parents away from the schools. Eleanor Brass and Georgina Gregory said that it was common to have the school quarantined to keep the parents from visiting at the school. The quarantine would last for months.[15]

At this time, the late 1800s, starvation and epidemics were decimating the Plains Cree tribal numbers across the prairies. After Fred's mother's death, Old Okanese travelled between the Cypress Hills and Turtle Mountain, where he died. As a result, Fred Dieter never returned to the Okanese band. School administrators considered him an orphan and he remained at the school until he was eighteen years old.

When he finally left the school, the Okanese band was not living the traditional lifestyle. The band no longer lived together but were divided into family units. Fred hired himself out to a local farmer, as was the practice for many young men who were leaving the schools.

William Graham, the Indian agent for the File Hills agency, was looking for recruits for an experiment he would later implement. It was called the File Hills Colony. Mr. Graham and others attempted to develop the ideal Indian community. His plan was to encourage marriage between the graduates from the industrial schools and settle them on a farming community of the Peepeekisis reserve. The first recruit was my grandfather.

At this time epidemics were causing great hardship for all Indians, including the children at residential school. Indian Affairs reported the mortality rate for the pupils at the File Hills school was 67.7 percent in 1907. Sarah Carter reports that in the first sixteen years of operation 75 percent of all the students who had been at the residential school were dead.[16]

The residential school experience continued with my parents. Both my mother Inez Deiter (Wuttunee) and my father Walter Deiter attended Indian residential schools from the age of eight until they were in their late teens. My mother attended both the Onion Lake school and the Prince Albert school in central Saskatchewan. Her interview is included in the book.

left to right, Mary Wuttunee, Inez Deiter, Loray Wuttunee on the stairs of the Onion Lake Indian Residential School, 1946

Walter Deiter, wearing the bow tie, and Eleanor Brass, seated third from right, at the Brandon Indian Residential School, 1931

My father Walter Deiter, now deceased, attended the residential schools at File Hills and in Brandon, Manitoba. During his lifetime, he spoke little to me about his residential school experience. He did mention that on the occasions when he ran away, he and the others would set traps for small animals. He told us the animals smelled so good roasting on an open pit. I can only imagine the hunger he felt if, forty years later, he fondly remembered the smell of roasting gophers.

He formed many strong beliefs as a result of attending these schools. For example, he would not eat mutton, not a morsel. He told us that when he attended the residential school in Brandon, they would feed the children rancid mutton. He also picked up some rather peculiar table manners. It would be frustrating at the dinner table when he insisted on not talking while seated. If he needed a condiment he would purse his lips and point in the general direction. We would be lifting everything placed on the table for his nod of acceptance. He just refused to ask for the salt.

My father developed lifelong friendships with the boys who attended the schools with him. These friendships later provided a foundation for his political activism as an adult. The camaraderie he found at the schools carried him through to his death. And finally, one of the reasons he moved his family into the city of Regina in 1950 was to prevent his children from attending residential school.

He did share one story about residential school with a family friend. He said that one day at the school, some men arrived to study Indian students. My father and some others were taken to a field far from the school. In the field, they were told to strip down while the men observed them. He told this family friend that they felt foolish and tried to cover their nakedness. These early social scientists just stood and watched them as if trying to determine whether the boys would go Indian again. He thought they were strange.

One last story illustrates further my father's attitude towards residential school. It happened when we were living in Regina. I had just returned home from lunch from my grade three class. I walked into the living room to find three white people sitting on our couch. My sisters and I were seated on the floor watching television when my father arrived home. He rarely came home for lunch, but that day he raced into the living room and chased out the white people sitting on our couch, all the time telling them to "get the hell out." I did not understand what was happening until years later. They were Indian Affairs staff and were there to take us to residential school. When I think about this incident I am reminded of the biblical story of Christ driving the moneychangers out of the temple, because when my father came into the room, his arms were swinging and he literally chased them out of our house.

Because so many generations attended residential schools they have affected all First Nations individuals. For example, even though I was raised in the city, all my family members, including my parents, my grandparents, uncles, and aunts on both sides of the family attended these schools. Most of my friends also attended the schools, including my husband and cousins. As well, all of the people whom my parents associated with during my formative years were residential school survivors. To say that the school experience did not directly affect my life would be a denial.

Part II
The Interviews

3

Eleanor Brass

Eleanor Brass is my paternal aunt and Fred Dieter's second daughter. Born in 1921, she was a life-long advocate for Indian people. In her role as advocate she took up a pen and wrote about her experiences, and the First Nations traditions of the File Hills Cree. Aunt Eleanor also became a historian and archivist; both she and my grandfather kept journals, scrapbooks, and photographs. Indeed, most of the remaining photographs of the File Hills agency came from their collection. In the late 1940s she began to write for several newspapers, including the Regina Leader-Post. *She published two books:* Medicine Boy and Other Cree Tales *and* I Walk in Two Worlds. *The following is an excerpt from* I Walk in Two Worlds. *It is published by the Glenbow Foundation in Calgary. Eleanor Brass attended the File Hills residential school from 1910 to 1920.*

When my sister Janet was seven years old and I was six, they put us into the Indian boarding school. Father wanted us to go to the white day school but the Indian agent said that it was compulsory for all Indian children to attend and live in the Indian school. It was approximately twelve miles from our home, but it seemed far away to us. At first we got terribly homesick and would cry ourselves to sleep at night.

The principal was Reverend H. C. Sweet; his name suited him for he was a very kind man. His wife was motherly to us and we loved them both very much; this made it easier for us to adjust. When Mr. Sweet went to town, we would wait patiently for him and when we saw him coming we would run out to meet him. We would pile into the buggy or sleigh and tell him what we did while he was away, and he would listen to us and act very interested.

There also was a matron to supervise the girls and to teach us housekeeping and sewing. Then there was a cook who taught the girls how to cook, bake, and do general kitchen duties. We used to mix large tubs of dough...my mother had taught us when we were old enough to reach the table by standing on a chair. Once in a while we had a trained nurse to look after our medical needs. I remember suffering with a terrible toothache; my jaw swelled up and I couldn't sleep at night. The nurse led me into the dispensary, took out her forceps, and told me to open my mouth. This was hard to do with a swollen jaw; however, she stuck this instrument in, probed around till she found the tooth, and kept yanking till it came out. It was unbearably painful, and I howled so loud they heard me all over the school.

At the school, I soon found out that if you were a favourite of any of the staff you could get away with a lot. But this was never my luck. It seemed that I was always getting into trouble and as a result I got a lot of strappings. That was something I really dreaded. The strap was sort of a heavy web rubber and did it ever hurt. It left large red welts on my arms and hands.

One day I got caught by one of the staff when I was passing notes. (The notes were passed to other sick children in quarantine.) I was taken into a locked room and there I was left all day with nothing to eat. I couldn't get to a toilet or bathroom, so I wet myself. I was about nine or ten years old. I dried my undies on the radiator and, of course, they gave off quite an odour. When the matron came to get me at night she smelled the odour and slapped me around for wetting myself, but I couldn't help it; there was no place to go.

She then took me up to the dormitory where the rest of the girls were in bed. She told me to get into my nightgown and lie across the bed on my stomach. Then she got a strap and strapped me on the back. Finally I got so numb that I couldn't cry anymore. But she kept on strapping me and telling the other girls that she was making an example out of me, and that they would get the same treatment if they got caught doing what I did.

The boys had their dormitory across the hall from ours and as there was a ventilator between us, the boys heard me howling. Pretty soon they were shouting at the matron to stop. Whenever any of us got into trouble we used to feel sorry for one another because the punishments were so severe.

There was a young boy at the school who was Chief Pasqua's son. He was about twelve years old, couldn't speak English, and was homesick because everything was so strange. Even his feet were blistered from having to wear leather shoes when he was used to soft moccasins.

He tried to run away but he was caught and brought back to school. Then the principal took him upstairs, made him strip and lie across the bed on his stomach, and started to strap him. We were all in our dormitory and began to bawl when we heard poor little John crying in pain till he couldn't cry anymore. Then someone called to the principal that his wife had fallen downstairs. He immediately stopped his strapping and ran downstairs saying "My poor Kate." That's when we all yelled "good, good," for it meant that he had finished with John. It seemed that when he started strapping anyone, he didn't know when to stop.

Poor John was raw and bruised from the back of his neck to his ankles. He couldn't bear any covers on his back for weeks. No doctor was called and no one except we children knew what went on. They used to quarantine the school in the winter time and our parents weren't allowed to come and see us. This is when we went through a lot of abuse and torture.

All my life I have suffered from a sore and tender back, which I attribute to the strappings I received in that school.

The principal's wife (not Mrs. Sweet) told us girls who were brought up in the File Hills Colony that we were no good because we couldn't speak Cree. Yet we weren't allowed to speak it anyway and would get strapped if we were caught. She was always picking on us.

Once when I needed a pair of shoes I went to see this matron.

"There are no shoes in the storeroom that will fit you," she said. "You will have to keep on wearing the shoes you have."

They were almost falling off my feet they were so broken and worn out.

One morning I came down late for breakfast when every-body else was in the dining room. On the way I saw the storeroom door partly open and I thought I would go in and investigate to see if there were any shoes that would fit me. However, I got caught by this matron who dragged me into the hall.

"You didn't believe me when I told you that there were no shoes that could fit you," she shouted at me. "Now I am going to get you a pair that will."

With that she brought out a pair of men's number nine buttoned boots and made me put them on. I was having a hard time buttoning them up but she stood over me until they were on. I had to wear these shoes, even though I used to trip and fall and had trouble keeping them buttoned up. Then they got so dry they turned up so that they made my feet even worse.

One time when we were lined up to go into the dining room, she noticed I didn't have my boots buttoned up. She made me step out of line and button them in front of the other children as they were passing by into the dining room. I was terribly embarrassed as the boys were all looking and snickering. It seemed as though I wore those old boots for a long time; it happened in the winter while we were in quaran-tine and my parents couldn't come and see me. If they had come, they would have given me a proper pair of shoes, I'm sure.

I had a cousin two years younger than me who ran away from school with a bigger girl. I felt at the time that she was forced by the other girl to go with her. When they were brought back to school they received a terrible strapping; their hands were swollen and looked like boxing mitts and their arms had huge welts. Then the principal chained my cousin's ankles together so that whenever she tried to walk she fell down. We were very sorry for her and tried to help her, but if we were caught we would get punished. It happened that my father (Fred Dieter) came to school just at that time to see us and when he saw my cousin, his face went white, he was so mad. He took the stairs in a few leaps right up to the principal's office, grabbed him by the scruff of the neck and dragged him downstairs to my poor cousin.

"Take those chains off that child!" he said, then he gave the principal a good shaking. "You're lucky this is all you're getting. These are children, not criminals and I don't ever want to see cruelty like this again."

We were glad to see my cousin happy again.

While I was at school, they kept barrels of apples in the attic. I don't remember them ever giving us any to eat so they must have been for the staff only. Somehow we found out about these apples so we discovered a way to steal them at night and take then to our beds to eat. The boys had easy access; they crawled across a small roof to the attic and took pillow cases to carry the apples back to their dorm. As each barrel became empty we turned it upside down.

One day a member of the staff went up get some apples and found all the barrels empty. Now we were in big trouble. We were all sent to bed immediately after supper and every night so many of us were called down to the office to get a strapping. When it came to my turn, I was scared.

"How many apples did you steal?" the principal asked.

I was hardly able to speak. "I don't know how many I stole," I said falteringly. "I think four or five."

"Oh, come on, you know you stole more than that," he said. "Hold out your hands."

He started strapping me and when I howled loudly, he laughed and said, "The Côtés are good singers." My mother had a fine voice and she had a cousin that was a professional singer.

Our meals at the school were always terrible. The porridge was either burnt or half cooked and I just couldn't eat it. Instead I gave it to my chum who said she didn't mind it. Whenever the supervisor caught me, she would make me eat it and I would nearly throw up. But she stood behind and hit me on the back, until I ate the last morsel. It never had sugar on it and the blackstrap they used for sweetening used to burn my tongue.

The dinners seemed to consist of watery soup with no flavour and never any meat. For supper we sometimes had dessert of a slice of bread and watery applesauce made out of dry evaporated apples. One winter we had fish every day for dinner; at first we enjoyed it but then we became tired of it.

They supplemented our diet with plenty of cod liver oil and iron but in spite of it, we seemed to be always sick and under-nourished.

We always had to take walks on Sundays and sometimes after school. This was nice in the summer time; we enjoyed picking flowers and looking for berries. In the latter part of the summer there were lots of nice ripe juicy rosehips, which we relished. We would pick a supply to take home in our pockets. But in the winter the walks weren't so pleasant; we were always dressed too lightly and used to suffer with the cold. Sometimes our toes would be frostbitten because we had no overshoes, only our leather boots and one pair of stockings. The staff didn't seem to worry if we were inadequately dressed to stand the winter weather. The tiny children would cry and wet their underclothes, which would soon be frozen stiff, and they would be spanked for it. The walks were quite an ordeal for children as we went about two or three miles at a time.

Some tragedies occurred while I was in school. Poor little Archie Feather fell through the ice in the early fall of 1913 or 1914 and was drowned. This made us all sad because we missed him very much. Another young man about seventeen years of age hanged himself. They found his body hanging from a beam in the barn. He was from the Carlyle Reserve. The poor youth was in some kind of trouble that wasn't so terrible but apparently it seemed that way to him. The staff could make it seem that way for they were always ready to deal out punishment. It was a very solemn time for us. It happened on a Sunday and we weren't allowed to leave our playrooms all day as the police were busy questioning the boys and the staff. Jack is buried on Peepeekisis reserve and his parents used to come every summer from the Carlyle reserve to visit his grave.

4

John Haywahe

John Haywahe is a respected elder from the Carry the Kettle reserve, eight miles south of Sintaluta, Saskatchewan. At the time of this interview, he was seventy-one years old. The interviewer is his daughter Brenda Haywahe.

I started school at the day school when I was ten. That time there was nobody to tell you when to start. I attended there for four years, then I went to the boarding school in File Hills when I was fourteen. The principal of the boarding school came for us by car in 1937.

There's lots of things that happened in the residential school. There was over 200 [students] altogether.

Saturday was our work day. The girls had the duties of doing laundry, baking and all that. They also made the bread.

Some of us [boys] sawed wood, chopped grain for the animals, and hauled wood for the woodpile to the school. Some guys looked after the barn and tend to the horses and cows. We looked after six horses and twenty milk cows. They also had to milk the cows. Some of the other chores the boys had was hauling out the ashes from the wood stoves and manure from the barn and from the chicken coop to the disposal grounds. They had their disposal grounds in a bush about half a mile from the school. This chore we did everyday. So that's the chores we had, everybody had his own way...

The meals were good. I ate porridge in the mornings and no toast...when dinnertime came around there was something like fish or chicken and potatoes. Oh, the meals were all right. We got to drink all the milk we wanted [laughs]. With twenty cows there'll be lots of milk! The girls made the butter. We called them "Dairy Girls" [laughs].

There was no breaks. We stayed there right through until June. Nobody even came to see us for Christmas, we stayed there from September until around the 28th or 29th of June. Each day we would mark it off on the calendar. Twenty-one more days...twenty more days...but today things are different.

There was six of us went to File Hills [in 1937] from here. Myself and my brother, Henry Ironstar, Fred Runns and his sister Leona, and Andrew Ryder. [We travelled in a] half-ton truck. Of course it had a cover at the back. A seat on each side [whistles]. [It took] about an hour I guess. An hour-and-a-half, that is straight north of Balcarres.

I went to the residential school for two years. After I turned sixteen I lived on the reserve with my parents. I was gonna go back to school but they said I had to stay home and work and the principal said that time if you want any help from me or the government we're supposed to let him know, ...I was supposed to tell the principal to help him, he never did though [laughs]. I was sixteen that time so I didn't go back. The principal was Charlie, or Frank, I think, Roades.

My family would sell wood or pickets. Wood in the wintertime. Everyday we'd take wood to town.To Sintaluta, Montmartre, Kendal. Three towns we go to. We go to each town everyday, cold days or not. A load of wood, walk behind it, let the horses just pull, follow the road... that's about all everybody had, school...residential school all alike, I think, according to the stories I hear. Some mean guys. [I experienced] a good licking sometimes. No, not too bad. I hardly ever got a licking. Just about sometimes, but I stand up for myself [laughs, taps on the table, and sniffs].

Robert and Theresa Bird

*Robert Bird is a respected elder from the Peepeekisis reserve, and a
decorated Second World War veteran. He has lived in southern
Saskatchewan for most of his life. At the time of this interview he and
his wife Theresa were living in Medicine Hat, Alberta. Robert at-
tended the File Hills Indian Residential School and the Brandon
Indian Residential School. Theresa attended the Catholic Indian
Residential School in Lebret, Saskatchewan. The interviewers were
Brian Gordon and Dean Puffault.*

Theresa: I was just about ten years old, I guess, or eleven. I
didn't go to school right away because dad used to keep us
back. We were supposed to be in school at a certain age. I guess
you know, but he didn't follow this. He always tried to keep
the kids back a bit. He didn't want to put us in right away because we were signed away until we were eighteen years old.
So that's a long time to be in school.

Which school would you have been signed away in?

Theresa: Oh Lebret school, Lebret Industrial school.

And who would sign you away for eighteen years? Who would
he sign with, was he signing with the Catholic school, with
Indian Affairs, who was he signing with?

Theresa: Oh sorry, I don't know that question because I think
it must have been a rule that all Indian kids had to go to

school and if you didn't put your kids in school, the police would...

Robert: ...lock them up.

Theresa: They were forced, we were being taken away from our parents.

What would happen to the parents if they interfered and tried to keep the children?

Theresa: Oh, I would imagine they would get into some kind of trouble with the Indian agent or the Indian affairs.

Did you ever hear of anybody actually protesting that their children be taken away?

Theresa: No, they did a lot of protesting but I don't remember anyone coming to that kind of problem. Later on, Thomas Stevenson, Stevenson girls went too, they were Protestants, but Tommy took them off. Now I don't know what school they went to but he put them in Lebret school for a while. Then, he took them out again. I think they went to Birtle school.

Robert: No, File Hills school. You see, I think there was a standing order right through Canada that all children had to go to school. These children had to go to school when they're seven years old. If you had them in before, it's all well and good but seven years was the kind of limit. All those kids had to go to school after that. Now what happened there, the Indian Department took that in their hands and they said all Indian children will, *will* go to school. They didn't want to go out to white schools or outside the reserve, that was out, strictly out. No way, we will build the schools and built them from Regina right through Canada. And these were big industrial schools and they were boarding schools and these children were taken from their parents, they were taken off the reserve and they were put in these schools. They didn't have any choice. There was no choice there at all. You go to school when you're seven years old and the priest and all these other people and the police and everybody were all involved in getting these kids into school.

And who, what type of people ran this? What kind of religion are you?

Robert: Well, you had your Church of England and your Catholics and the United Church and before that it was called the Protestant schools. Your main ones was your Catholics and your Protestants. We used to call them Anglicans, my mother went to an Anglican school, my father went to a Protestant school, and I started out in a Protestant school but eventually we changed over to the United Church.

What was a typical day like in school?

Robert: It was—you mean what it was like to be a student in the school?

Yeah, like when you woke up, what happened and during the day and in school? What type of things were you guys taught?

Robert: Yeah well, listen it was kind of an industrial background to the whole thing. You got up in the morning and you helped with the chores. You milked the cows, you fed the horses and the pigs, or whatever you had and this is the first assignment before breakfast. Second, was lining up for breakfast. You all came in, got washed, washed your hands and face, and then went to breakfast. You lined up for that. You see, you didn't walk into a dining room, there was no such thing. Everything was very military [laughter].

After the breakfast, you might have played for maybe twenty minutes to half an hour, then you were into a classroom. You went to school, class work there. The classroom was from grade one to grade eight. Well, these were the people that went to school in that time and in the afternoon half of the class, half of that class I'm talking about went to school. The boys worked out on farms or out in the buildings, whereas the girls, they baked bread and did domestic work like sewing and things like that. They were taught that and then maybe a couple of weeks after they changed over. They went to class in the mornings you see, and so therefore, your education wasn't the prime thing, and I think what they're trying to do was to get you know how to farm, how to sew, how to cook, and you know, some places it was good. I think I learned a lot but I didn't learn too much about farming because File Hills wasn't noted for being a good farm, put it that way, but when I went to Brandon that was a whole different thing.

Okay, one more question about your day. What time of the day did you guys get up and what time did it finish and were you always under supervision and that type of thing?

Robert: Yeah, well the ones that went out and got the cattle, got the cattle in and the horses in, they might have to go out at 5:30 you know.

Was there someone who walked in and said "Okay, it's time to get up"?

Robert: Oh, yeah, yeah [laughter], they did, they did come. They came in yelling and screaming [laughter], banging on the beds, and everything like that. Then they got the bigger ones or whoever was assigned to getting the cattle in and then the other boys came along with them, but there it was all milked by hand.

Before I went to school we lived up at the west colony, what we called the west colony. I come from the File Hills colony, by the way, and we lived at the west colony. Dad come back from the war in 1918. He had a start of a little farm. He had four horses and just a very small farm, then had problems there with the size of the land or something, didn't have quite enough land for what he wanted to do so we moved. We traded to the middle colony.

When I became seven years old they were going to have to put me in school there when we were at this middle east colony there. I used to have to ride to school, five miles, when I was just six-and-half-years old, but I had my own horse. I was a pretty good horseman when I was six years old and I used to ride to school. It was pretty cold, a day like this would be really killing, I tell you [deep breath] but 25 or 30 below [Fahrenheit], blowing, and it would be pretty cold but I made it for two years. I always remember when I was a bit younger than six and a half, there used to be wide open land. You can't imagine how it is today, everything all farming and everything like that. At that time, it was wide open. You've seen pictures of the wide open prairies, okay, that's what I lived on. I went to the Lorlie school for two years and during the thirties things were starting to get pretty tough then and dad was having a hard time and we were all having a hard time. So dad decided to put me into boarding school, at least there's one less mouth to feed.

So I went to File Hills until 1930, and I had my grade eight and then I had to go on, because there's no higher grade, like you remember I said it was from one to eight. This is one thing I'll say, there was a difference between Protestants and Catholics. The Catholics didn't have a higher grade, a higher schooling. We had the opportunity to go to high school, so we went to Brandon, Manitoba. So I took my grade nine in Brandon the first year, and then I went on and took tech for three years there. When I got out of there, after completing that, I graduated, I got an honourable diploma [laughter].

6

Bette Spence

Elizabeth Spence is the leading elder at Saskatchewan Indian Feder-
ated College in Regina. She is from the Red River Reserve, north of
Prince Albert, Saskatchewan. She was interviewed by Zena Wiest
and Melissa Lerat.

I was born on the Little Red River reserve. It's about 32 miles
north of Prince Albert and I attended residential school in
Brandon for six or seven years. It was during the dirty thirties
and our little day school only went up to grade three or four,
so to go further that we had to go somewhere else. It was a
one-room school and it was, well most of the students didn't
have any word of English. You know, they had to learn right
from the bottom up. But I was kind of fortunate in that I
learned how to speak English when I was four years old, but
up to then nothing but Cree.

In the residential school I was not really allowed to speak
Cree, but they didn't know 'cause we just switched to English
every time we saw a supervisor coming or something like that.

There was not one single native tradition in the school.
They just took you away from home, where you left everything, all the Indian-ness back there. They took you where all
the supervisors were all white people.

How long did you go to school for in the year?

Bette: You went home for your two months, sometimes just
six weeks. We had Christmas right on the residential school,

we had Christmas, I mean a tree, a Christmas tree and some. Christmas Day was one time of the year that they gave us turkey, just the one time of the year. Turkey, I don't remember the pudding or anything, but I remember the turkey and potatoes and gravy.

How were your trips home? Did you enjoy going home for your two months?

Bette: Oh, of course. We had to get home sometime, but we were all herded into a truck with wooden benches. Imagine driving on those for, well from Brandon to Prince Albert is eight to nine hours, bumping along on those beautiful benches.

The whole world was ours, when we got home. All the countryside and the animals and it was nice to go horseback riding and everything else like that. And go fishing somewhere. It was real nice, real relaxing.

I had two, three sisters went to the same, same area that I went to and another sister went to File Hills. So, we weren't always all together. I didn't communicate anywhere. If we went anywhere at all it would be to church on Sundays, right in the city. So that was our outing and it didn't come very often. I had to rotate on the duties we did. And we only went to school half a day. So for us dumb ones we didn't learn too much you know. Going to school was half a day and the rest of the day we did housework. Helping to clean pots and pans in the kitchen, and mending, and so on in the sewing rooms. Darning. All those domestic duties.

The boys gardened and everything else and they looked after the farming and so on. And one thing about it, you know, they grew their own meat but mostly sheep. And that wasn't very, not at all inviting to see the gruel, always looked like that thing there. The stew [laughs and points to a floor mat]... The grey part on top of the floor. Yeah, and it was never tasty. Just bits of lamb floating in this white, off-white gravy, you know. So it was really, it wasn't appetizing at all. But, you had to eat something or just go hungry.

I think that was the only time where we really ate [was at home] you know. One of my sisters is a very good cook. And she used to bake. She'll start Wednesday baking and so on. My father had a truck and we'd pick up people along the way and go to a picnic or something you know. Create your own sports day and so on, and by the time you got over there it was dinnertime and everybody was out in the field playing ball or football. That was our outing during those days. But there was also gardening, picking weeds, and not getting paid for it you know. Long rows of gardens.

Did you eat fresh vegetables?

Bette: Not at the hospital. Not at the residential school. We did have potatoes. I don't remember any other vegetable except for maybe onion in the darn lamb stew. You know, it wasn't appetizing at all.

So what happened to the vegetables that came from the garden?

Bette: That's the part I don't know. I've been trying to remember what they did with them. So they must have stewed them. Most of the time they put them in the stew. Stew all the time. We just seemed to have stew all the time. On Sundays it was kind of special. They would have roast and potatoes and things you know, but that's about it. The most stewing place you ever came across you know [laughter]. Sometimes for dessert [we had] rice pudding or tapioca you know. And to this day I don't eat tapioca. "Oh, you're going to eat fish eyes you know," and we'd always say, "Yuck."

Did you attend church at all?

Bette: Yes, we had chapel everyday and on Sundays we attended church right in the city. We rotated people, that's the way it was. I kind of enjoyed that because it took me out of the building and took me off the grounds. Went to church and we used to have a choir leader and she spent time with us singing and singing you know, and that was good part of it because we, the whole choir, they were all Indians. We won three trophies, one after another, three years in a row. So that was, that was good for us, it did our morale very, very good, just enlightening us. That's was one good point, you know, something to remember.

We had hardly any free time. And it was a darn good thing we didn't, because I think we'd be bored out of our wits if we had any free time you know. Although we had reading and so on, and every meal if you weren't washing dishes or something, you'd get locked in the playroom, what we call the playroom. Especially in wintertime because we couldn't go outside. We didn't have the clothing to begin with to go outside. Overshoes and things like that, so we really didn't so we had to stay in.

During the war, they had war surplus coats and so on, army coats and so on. And they hired a dear little old lady to make everybody a coat out of those. Very new coats you know, mind you, but we all looked alike. They might have just as well left in the original style and so on, because the colour didn't change. All khaki colours. We sewed our own clothes. We looked like the Michelin man. Our underwear was made out of unbleached cotton with elastic bands here and puffy you know. I don't remember how we ever kept our stockings up. We used to have stockings, maybe it was elastic in the pantaloons.

Do you remember getting in any trouble for anything? Any particular thing?

Bette: Oh, it was such an unnecessary trouble we got into. One time we were all, we belonged to a group of what you would call CGIT—Canadian Girls in Training—and every year we used to join the girls in the other churches across the city, and this one time we were invited out, the whole group was invited out to a banquet and what do we have, beans. A bean supper and they called it a banquet. I don't even remember what dessert we got. Anyway, one day there was two truckloads of girls. First truckload went to the right place and the second truckload had a different driver and he just dumped us at any old church...he was too far away for us to even call back that this was the wrong church. But anyway, he dumped us there.

And here we walked and walked. I don't know we must have walked for over an hour to get to the other church. And our guide, one of the senior girls, kept saying "I think it's over here." Oh, it just seemed as if we would never get there. And I wasn't a very good walker because I was, I got one gimpy leg I should say. So anyway, I followed along.

And the next thing we all got hauled in, "Why did you do that? Why did you do that?" Oh boy did he ever give us the most terrible looks. We just got dumped in the wrong place, so she made a big issue out of it as if we had done it on purpose. "Why did you do this?" Oh, big toad. We called him big toad because he was such a broad man you know, and stubby little fingers, they're just about half the size of mine. Big, fat sausage fingers you know, and he looked like a toad. He had a little moustache and a big, fat face, and very little hair and he always swung this over this way, you know. It just, I don't know how he ever kept it up there. But, anyway he called us one at a time and, "I'm sorry to do this. Why did you do, why did you delay the whole banquet? They were waiting for you," and all this. Well, we didn't know, we just went along. But anyway he brought the strap out. He'd look at you in the face and come down with that strap on your hands you know, and I didn't wince or anything. But I looked on his desk when he'd bring the strap down. "I hate to do this but I got to." Well, he always pretended to have a crying voice you know. Oh my goodness, too. "This hurts me more than you know." So, anyway, I walked, walked out. He didn't call me back but he called me back in the next morning. And again the same thing, "Why'd you do that?" So I just stood there now, "What did I do you know?"

"Oh, you hurt me when you stabbed that knife into my heart."

So I got quite defensive. I said, "What knife?"

I'm being stupid now because I thought for sure he was. You've got to be crazy. "What knife?"

"Oh, that knife that you stabbed into my heart. It just hurt me terribly," he said.

And I thought to myself, you dare come near me and just within my reach of that, of that heavy letter opener you know, and he backed up, he backed away. He didn't come any closer. So after that he treated me as if I was, almost a lady. I'm sure I would have hit him with that thing. Because it just gets you like that, because you know there's nobody there to defend you, you have no rights of any kind.

They read every bit of mail that you got and they read every bit of mail that you sent out. And they called me one day about something I said in a letter. I said they are just allowing some of the students just to steal, 'cause there was one girl was always doing something like this. She'd go in the staff rooms and take something and everybody else would get the blame for it. And one day this girl, I don't know what but, she took something of mine. Anyway, I wrote it all down in this letter. And I said they're just allowing this girl to do all this stuff and she's always stealing from the rooms and so on. So I got called in, and she said, "I'm not going to send this."

"That's fine," I said, "I don't send it, you don't have to send it," and I said "I won't write another letter."

Because we were allowed one a letter a month. I said I won't write another letter so I walked out and they did send it. And my father wrote back a very, just a beautiful letter. It just took me off my own case you know, and just made me feel good. Because there are some people that are like that because they have nothing. So that was fine, and I think they must have read that letter too, because they didn't bother me after that. But it's surprising, how all of these little things have happened.

But there was one staff, my goodness. This one staff, she was very good to the kids, the students. She was the laundry mistress. She, every time you went in there for something, she'd have a loaf of bread and jam and peanut butter. Oh, this is great working for this department you know, the laundry department, because we used to have a big long line up of students ironing, ironing our bloomers, so they wouldn't be so rough you know, our brassieres, slips, dresses, but sometimes we had to iron the staff dining room, white tablecloths. We had to iron them a certain way. But this lady always, halfway through the morning, would bring in a loaf of bread and peanut butter and jam. It was delicious. She was very good to us.

But one time there, on her holidays, she went to the States and she came back and gave the matron a necklace. And she, none of us had ever seen it. But one day, one morning the whole group of girls got hauled into the assembly hall. "Now which one of you did it?" So we all sat back, everyone of us. Now what's wrong? "You'll stay here until you confess." Now what were we to confess to, you know? We sat down and all the staff sat over there. And this lady had Parkinson's Disease. She went like this all the time, jiggling all the time. She had a good heart for the students and we didn't mind that one bit. But anyway, it came about. We must have been there two hours maybe longer to fess up. And we were all bugging, "Why don't you confess?" Why, don't you?, all down the line. "Well I didn't do that. Say something so we can get out of here." But we didn't, we sat there like dummies, and it's a good thing we sat there, eventually they let us all off you know, to go to dinner.

Anyway, we go called in again and this poor lady has been stealing gas from the gas pump all this time and she must have been with the Indians too long, she took back the necklace. She stole it back, the necklace that she gave to this lady. So that's what came about, you know she stole it back. But there were no apologies, "Sorry to keep you here all the time." There was no apology like that.

And you couldn't speak to your brother on the other side or your cousin, whoever. If you were caught talking to a boy, any boy, you'd get your hair cut right off. What was wrong with talking to the boys? It's a darn wonder we, any of us even got married. Because it was a sin to talk to a boy. Good grief.

Were you in class with boys, too?

Bette: Yes, but it was under supervision at all times. We had a recess but our own section. Sometimes we didn't have, we just went clear through right until dinner time. And sometimes, you know, especially Sundays, you'd have all afternoon 'cause you're not going to school. You'd just walk around the little park that we had, within sight of the classroom so nobody would run away. As if they'd like to because by the time afternoon came you were so darn tired from hunger, you just had no energy left. But anyways, some of us used to just sit under the oak trees and these acorns would fall down. Then we would pretend that they were nuts and they were very nice you know. They tasted good. And sometimes when the boys were picking tomatoes and digging potatoes and all that, they'd be throwing these tomatoes at us and green tomatoes. Oh they were good, good to eat. It was just a great treat. But the only thing that they never threw at us were carrots. Now those, those would have been a real treat.

Well anyway, you know, it's all in our lifetime, an awful lot of us went to day school on the reserve then, then right straight to residential school. And we went through the same thing all over again you know, for six years or so you know getting picked up and taken to school. Going to school half day and working the rest of the time, house cleaning and everything else. Working in the kitchen. It wasn't a very pleasant place that kitchen, because the cook seemed to be always mad. Big, bony cook. What did we call her? Bottle legs. "Look at old bottle legs." Milk bottle legs, that's what we called her. So it was everybody had a pet name, Toad especially. He was a real toad you know. A real human toad. Little things like that. Not once did we have an Indian for our supervisors or anything. Not one. And it's so sad because you know those little girls that come in some of them, five and six years old. They'd be crying you know, some of them eventually they'd be so lonesome that they'd wet their beds and so on. And we were assigned, a couple of the big girls were assigned to look after these little girls. And you know, dry their mattresses somehow and send them down with their sheets to get washed and everything. It was quite a chore you know, but it sure made you think twice about how to help these girls because they were crying.

And I've always said how it is that these white people who have never had families of their own and looking after little ones that came in. They couldn't talk to them or even pat them. "You're okay, you're doing fine, don't be lonesome," or anything like that. These little girls used to cry and cry. And if there was an overflow there, they'd have one of the girls come into the senior dorm and this little one would be crying all night, keeping everyone awake. Mind you, but you could understand why they were crying. It was sad that way, very sad. Those little ones you know, taken away from home, brought to school. But eventually they all had, more or less, all had big sisters. We took it upon ourselves to look after these kids.

What do you think the effect of residential schools has been on Indian people?

Bette: The effect. Well, in a lot of cases real negative because when they take you away from your own home, you know how that feels and you can't get back, back and forth. And I'm sure that's what some of these students feel here [at Saskatchewan Indian FederatedCollege—Regina campus]. Because they are so far away from their parents and so on, you know, from their home life. It does crowd you. It starts to wear you down a little bit you know and you have to remind yourself what you are here for and so on. I've got to go to school, got to go to school. That's a matter of survival really. Then the ten months isn't so far away, when you think of it as ten months from now, you can go home then and just enjoy the summer. And the effect on them, I think that's really quite negative because when you graduate from residential school you don't have a ready made home or anything like that. You're on your own, you have to start all over again, recognizing who's around you and so on. It's quite damaging because you don't know who you left at home. Sometimes your mom and dad are strangers and your little brothers and sisters are all brand new to you and you have to learn all over again, how to be a big sister or whatever. And it's that way if you didn't have that background, and you left it behind. It's a real learning experience. You have to learn all over again. And you have to learn to love and take it and if you criticize someone, you have to learn to take criticism also. And you have to respect whoever, you know, but that, even the four years or six years you're at home with that bit of background from your mom and dad, to respect somebody or something or anything. It's always there so you know, you have to build that up again.

7

Inez Deiter

Inez Deiter is from the Peepeekisis Indian reserve in Southern Saskatchewan, but she was born and raised at the Red Pheasant reserve in the North Battleford region. She attended the Onion Lake Indian Residential School and the Prince Albert Indian Residential School as a child from 1938 to 1946. Her memories are typical of the experiences of children attending the school. She is in her early sixties. I interviewed her; she is also my mother.

I was born on the Red Pheasant reserve in a little log cabin in 1931 or 1932. I was raised on the reserve until my mother separated from father and took me to a Métis settlement in Alberta called Fishing Lake.

Tell me a little about your education, did you attend primary school? Day school?

Inez: Nothing, in those days there was not anything like that. There wasn't a day school, that was in the thirties. Everyone was poor, the Métis people were really poor. The people I used to stay with didn't have floors. I remember Joe Pareanteau, they were very, very good to me. My mother died when I was four years old. I lived with the Métis until I was eight years old. My stepfather took me to an orphanage-convent in Edmonton.

Then the people in Red Pheasant were looking for me, but my mother changed my name to Letendre. A relative in

Edmonton spotted me, Jesse Latta, told my people in Red Pheasant. My people made arrangements for me. I don't remember too much about the orphanage. There were white girls there. Then one day a nun called me in and told me that I was an Indian and not a Letendre. That I had relatives and I had a father in Red Pheasant reserve. Your people want you, so they put me on the train and someone met me at Lloydminister. A Sam Decouteau met me, then took me to the Onion Lake School. They took me straight to the school.

My first contact was with my relatives, Freda, Gladys, Florence, and my cousin Willie, and my brother Maurius. I remember my cousin Florence spent all night trying to tell me my name was Inez Wuttunee. She was teaching me how to spell the name Wuttunee. I said no, I was not Inez. I was stubborn because I thought I was a real Roman Catholic and my name was Mary. They told me there was already another Mary Wuttunee and you have to stick with Inez. That was my first contact with my relatives. They were happy to meet me.

I got there [my first day at school] at night. I was ashamed to undress in front of my cousins. They were so fed up with me, so my cousin Gladys threw me in clothes and all. The gave me some charcoal to brush my teeth. I had a tooth brush and a towel. I remember the supervisor gave me a number; it was 142. It was the number I would use all through boarding school. It was more or less adjusting from the convent to learn my relatives.

The next day they told me I had a brother. I went upstairs. They called it a parlour where people would go and visit. I remember seeing Maurius for the first time since I was a little girl. I saw this man Maurius, he was fifteen then. He had big tears in his eyes when he saw me. He told me, "Gee, you ugly." That's the first thing he told me cause we looked exactly alike. He was teasing me about my freckles. He was happy to see me. He told me about my Dad. He found out I couldn't speak Cree, and he knew that was going to be a problem. The first word he taught me was *mistick*, and that was for a stick. And then I knew that my Dad didn't speak Cree and my relatives all spoke Cree, so I knew I had to try and grasp some of this Cree. I heard the girls speaking Cree and I would copy them. The Cree was forbidden to be spoken at the school, so they would teach me on the *kimooch* (sly) at night. We would sit up and the girls would teach me Cree. I noticed that everything was secretive, and that's what I found out when I went there. Everything was secretive.

I soon learned the ropes. We didn't have enough to eat. We were given jobs. At nine years old I didn't have as many jobs. I was kind of daring. They always made me—I'd be the one to go into the pantry. The big girls would go work in the staff dining room. They would come up with butter. They would steal butter. And we used to be hungry at night. I remember going to the bakery and I stole a loaf of bread. We used to wear bloomers and I stuck the loaf and raced up the stairs. I was kinda a hero after that 'cause we all shared this bread and butter and whatever we could get. It was really hard. We learned to be on the sly, secretive, because I noticed that they would all keep quiet when the supervisors would come in. I didn't have any problems like a lot of girls had with cultural experiences, where they had to have their braids cut off and all these stories about them wearing moccasins and having to fit into white man's shoes. I didn't have those problems because I knew these things from the convent. We were treated okay.

The Cree was what I was really interested in. I learned how to speak Cree at residential school. I made a lot of friends there. I was very friendly. I don't remember getting beaten up, I was kinda a ham, kinda leader.

A month after I started at the school, we were going back to our reserves. All the girls were excited, they got their little treasures, little suitcases, little gym bags, but I didn't have anything. My supervisor felt sorry for me, so she gave a nice box to go home with. There was nothing in there except chocolate wrappers, and that is what I took home with me, and maybe a few clothes that were given to me. We went on a truck, we were all put in the back. The truck was covered, and there were benches. I remember sitting with my brother and he was busy trying to teach me Cree. He was trying to prepare me for home. My cousins were all excited about what they were going to do for the summer.

When we got to Red Pheasant my dad was there and a lot of people were there to welcome me because they hadn't seen me for years. And the Cree was a problem. They were talking to me in Cree and Maurius was talking to me. He was my interpreter. My Dad said I looked like my mother and that I had freckles. They did not know what to do with me because I only spoke English. So they put me with Eli, my oldest brother. He was established with a wife and two kids, and lived in a log house. I remember meeting with my brother. I remember he was so happy to see me. I know he loved me and my other brothers came, Sam and Harry. It was a homecoming and it was nice. I learned to pick up a few words in Cree by the end of the summer.

Then it was time to go back to school. Maurius was not going to go back this time. Auntie Gladys and Eli put some clothes together for me. They took me back to school, and I started adjusting. When you were little you don't see all those things, but then as time went I heard, my ears were always open for Cree. They would talk about their summers. I spent time with Auntie Nancy's mother, she was a medicine women. When I would go and visit she would say in Cree, "a gift." Like my presence was a great gift to her. That's the way those old people used to be. They were so very nice.

Then it dawned on me that things were not the way they should be. I was becoming sneaky too, lying, in order to survive, we had to do these things. We used to lie and I think all those ten commandments that we were taught when we were in church all the time. We learned to be soldiers. That was nice. I used to like the band. But the roughness I didn't like, the supervisor was rough. The principal was rough, Mr. Ellis. He used to strap the girls. I remember I ran away one time. He told us to undress and put our nightgowns on and take this great big web strap. He would give us strappings; we would see the foam on his mouth. He used to get so mad, maybe close to a heart attack. He used to do the strappings. I remember I was kinda like a leader then. I noticed the little girls being abused. I remember I spoke out in line. We used to have to line up in a great big dining room. I remember we used to have a great big dining room. We fought for survival from the other girls. They would beat us up if we did not watch our p's and q's. So we had to resort to our relatives. I would have to look to our kinship to look after me. After Freda and Gladys left, there was Florence. We were kinda close, and we would look after each other. After Florence left, I had to be kinda tough for survival. I would help the younger girls who would be getting beat up by the other students. Of course we were all put together.

There was the junior, intermediate, and senior girls. By the time I was a senior girl, I was getting to be hard, and taking up for the junior girls and in order to survive we had to resort to a lot of things that were not normal. Then after a while you become bitter and you blame things. One instance, I would get mad when I went out with the little girls and we would go out on the playground. Most of my trouble was my big mouth. I would get mad when I would see the little girls outside in the winter time with wet pants. They wouldn't let them in to go to the washroom during the times we were to be outside. Not enough clothes, warm clothes. It was to become that way. I guess that is why Indians today look after one another because they had to survive. I became a big sister to a lot of those young girls. I remember one time talking out of line and the supervisor came and slapped me really hard on the face in front of everybody.

And another time Miss Hover, she was great for hitting kids on the ears, cuffing them. At that time, I had a running ear, neglect. No one bothered to take me to the hospital to get it looked after. She used to cuff me on the ear and say, "You silly little hussy." She used to call us down. These supervisors, this was during the war. They were not qualified, they were just there for the money. Consequently I got into a lot of trouble because I used to speak out. And today now, I can't hear. I'm deaf. Both my eardrums are damaged, and I have to wear a hearing aid. I always think that was from neglect. The girls used to have toothaches and they would suffer.

I think that the generation that Auntie Eleanor went through was terrible, the days before us. When we went it wasn't too bad, except for being hungry and not having enough clothes to wear in the winter. It was survival, but we used to have to learn to steal and lie, and be sneaky. I remember we used to tease each other, we used to have boyfriends, etc.

But the girls used to have girlfriends, boyfriends, passing notes in school. I remember one case while I was there at school. I think it was Georgina Vandel and Bertha Sanqui. They ran off, Bertha Sanqui's boyfriend was Tommy Bird, she eventually married him. And Georgina Vandel with Noel Wuttunee, my cousin. They ran off together. They were about fourteen and fifteen. After they were apprehended, they were brought back, and their heads were shaved, all their hair was gone. This was close to summer holidays and we were all so shocked.

I don't know who brought them back. I think the night watchman. We used to go in the truck, there was a lot of staff working there. Maybe someone reported them. I ran away too, in Prince Albert. It was dangerous, there was a ledge running outside the building; it was three stories high. We left through a window and outside on the ledge until we got to the fire escape. But I know lots of people who ran away, even this man Victor McNab. He ran away three times. He used sheets to get out. There were reasons that people ran away. Maybe if you don't get your way I guess. We all had to conform. A lot of it was the abuse others were suffering. Morale was very low. It was depressing. People would complain about the food. The food wasn't very good, watery porridge, and applesauce, mutton, and we didn't care for those. While I was in Onion Lake somebody burned the school down. It was in January and in the night. We were all put on trucks and sent to the Roman Catholic school at Onion Lake. I told them, I always used my wits. I said I was a Roman Catholic, then I was treated a little better. We were then sent back to the reserve.

I guess I could say the bitterness was brushed off on us. It was dull, it wasn't a happy place. Now, I think of little zombies. Us you know little zombies, like little puppets, not like today. Kids can do whatever they want. Over there you had to do it. One thing that came out is that today I find myself very rigid, doing things making sure they are done quick. I find myself jumping. I learned to become very anxious. That was part of our training from the boarding schools, and always finding a way to cope, even if it meant lying. We had to resort to devious methods for survival. I remember going home when I was fifteen. I remember I was always smart and good in school.

After the school burned in Onion Lake they found another school for us in Prince Albert, St. Alvins. It was right across from the high school. I remember getting into a fight there. They were two sisters. That is what we had to do was to fight, take up for one another. We learned our culture from each other. We knew lots about different things. One time a girl said she was going to make it rain. She showed me how to do it, but when I went home and showed my relatives, they laughed at me. They taught me about the Round Dance, and the northern lights. One time in Prince Albert we were all sitting in the dorm. One girl said if you whistle, the northern lights they will come to you. Someone whistled and suddenly you heard a "whoosh" and everybody crawled under their bed.

We weren't taught to be kind and gentle, we were taught to be rough except when we went back to the reserve. It was nice to go home to the reserve. One time I went to a Sundance, not to participate but just for the joy of seeing other students from the school. Already we were like brothers and sisters, forming a kinship because we were together ten months out of the year. This would be the time we would talk about our experiences at residential school. This would be the time we would tell our secrets from the school. Like it was the time for holidays, and this person had about four boxes of stuff to take home. So the supervisor asked her to open the boxes in front of all of us, and discovered that she was taking home sheets from the school. And she really embarrassed the girls. We were taught by public humiliation. Like the students that ran away, they had to go to school like that. They had to sit in the front of the class as if to say this is what will happen to you if you run away.

Bertha and Tommy did eventually get married and this was a real experience to them. I found out from that experience we were not really honest. We were taught to be deceitful, never honest. That beauty was taken from us, that innocence that caused us to be hard. We knew we were different from the white people, so consequently, when it came time to assimilate with them I couldn't stand them. I just couldn't even when I had my children, and there were PTA meetings. I would stay away, not realizing I was hurting my children. But just for the fear, because we were treated as if we were not accepted. I remember when we went to Prince Albert school. Freda knew how to act with white people, this was a stumbling block for us. Pretty well all of us were that way. We never had any love, or nurturing, mothering. My father was kinda cold. My friends were those in boarding school. I went to visit a friend a few years ago. The one I ran away with, she remembered how we walked all night to Duck Lake from Prince Albert. There was timber wolves and everything. When we got back we got a strapping.

I liked the kinship of the schools, but to prepare us for life, for our own families, we didn't know nothing, we didn't know any parenting skills. Those who didn't go to residential school had it much better. So some people say the residential school was all right. It was okay if you had enough relatives to keep an eye on you to take care of you. But those that didn't they had it pretty rough. They were being abused. There was no one there to take up for them. And if they had a strong family back home they would be looked after, the supervisor would look after them, treat them better. But not if they had nobody and didn't know anything, didn't know how to speak English, and no relatives. One little boy was there when he was four years old. His parents died, he had nowhere to go. He never got any loving, he needed a mother, and he was with the boys. He turned out to be a severe alcoholic. We always asked about him, and still ask about him because we remember when he was just a little kid and having nobody.

What about this sign language, you learned at residential school ?

Inez: What we used to do was sign language. I learned that quick, it was the British form of signing. It was a common thing for everybody, when they wanted to get [information]. We weren't allowed to speak in class, in the dining room, and in church. We used to have to use this sign language to communicate. So were learned another language.

How many hours a day would you not be talking?

Inez: Oh I don't know, church, sometimes early in the morning, make our beds, go to church, then for breakfast, then go and do our chores, washing, scrubbing floors, working in the laundry, working in the bakery. The supervisor would make our work orders. We all wanted to work in the bakery and the dining room because that meant food. We weren't allowed to speak in boarding school, in church, in the dining room. If we were caught we were slapped, strapped, or humiliated in some way, so consequently we learned this sign language. It came in handy.

I don't know who taught me, I just picked it up. But, anyway years later, I was going to university, and I thought of quitting the second year. Then I went to visit my friend Rosenna, we attended residential school together. There used to be special treatment given to those students who went to high school; we were allowed to sit in the dining room, etc. There weren't very many of us, maybe five. The other students from the school did not attend high school, and they were stuck doing the hard work. Rosenna was one of those, she worked as a janitor. She reminded me of that. She said she was not ashamed of it, but the staff used to make a fuss over the high school girls. So, after that I went back to university to finish because I felt I owed it to them.

8

Ben Stonechild

Ben Stonechild attended the File Hills school on the Okanese reserve. The band that lives on this reserve, northeast of Balcarres, is one of the bands that make up the File Hills agency. The school was operated by the Presbyterian Church, then by The United Church of Canada. Ben Stonechild was attending the school when it closed in 1949. He is interviewed by Constance Deiter.

That residential school was something that I cannot say anything bad about. The only thing bad I could say about it was that we felt we never got enough to eat. As kids we were always on the move. Always seem to be looking for something extra to eat, and if the cook left bread out to cool, boy we would get it. For breakfast we would eat porridge mostly. We ate a lot of raw vegetables, like carrots. We may have got a little meat, now and then. It's been such a long time since I've been there.

We always done something to get something extra to eat. It was nothing for the boys to go behind the chicken house and shoot a chicken. Take off in the bush, we had pails out there, different places. Go and cook our chicken up. We had salt to cook. We were lucky. Saturdays and Sundays we went hunting rabbits with our sling shots.

I think if we ever shared with the girls they cooked the rabbit. It was quite the thing, there would be a lot of boys. When we used to go out Sundays hunting rabbits. Someone

would say "a rabbit, a rabbit, surround him, surround him."
Away we would go, that rabbit never stood a chance. We were
about nine or ten years old. We would shoot it with a sling-
shot. We get a bunch and trade it for bannock on the weekend,
trade it with the older people who would come to visit on the
weekend. They always brought lots of bannock because they
knew we always had rabbits. [It was] a treat you know. Sometimes the boys who lived near the school would run home on
weekends. Sometimes boys would be lucky enough to run
home with them. They would get bannock there.

When I think back about it, they were the best years of
my life, even at the time we thought they were tough, but we
weren't molested in any way at the schools. It wasn't like the
stories you hear at other places. I say we were treated good, it's
kind of surprising to have to say that. When you hear of all
the injustices at other boarding schools. I would say we were
fortunate in that we didn't have to go through what other
schools, other children had to go through.

How old were you when you started?

Ben: I was raised in Drumheller, Alberta, East Coulee. My father was a coal miner, there. In 1944 or 1943, they brought me
to boarding school, they lived down there [East Coulee]. I
might have went home on holidays to my uncle Harry
Stonechild. Most of the time I spent at the boarding school. I
can't recall, I think my dad moved back in 1945. When he
moved back, we had to work hard, even in the boarding school
we had to work hard. We all had jobs, chores to do, wood to
cut. We burnt wood all winter. One of the things, it kind of
got cold in there, wintertime, but we survived. I guess it was
healthy for us.

We had one death in there when I went to school. There
was some kind of a strange sickness that they couldn't do
nothing about. A young boy, he was quarantined and all the
windows and doors were kicked shut.

You were the last to attend the File Hills residential school?

Ben: All of us guys like me and Keith [Dieter], Grant [Dieter]
and Joey Ironquill. We were the last, they built a school down

in our district [Peepeekisis], they closed the boarding school. I wish they would have kept it open, at least we could have had a landmark, some history, etc. We had some boys in there that rebelled and burnt down part of it. I guess [the] late Jimmy [name not supplied] had something to do with the burning. It was rebuilt, you could not tell where the fire was. I guess it was a routine thing, it wasn't a change thing.

I know one time a boy supervisor went out hunting with the boys with a twenty-two. He made a mistake, well I wouldn't say he made a mistake. He wouldn't let the boys take a turn at the twenty-two. So they got him and tied him up, then they got the twenty-two and used it. That happened with the senior boys, it was kind of the talk around there at that time. My uncle Chappie was one of them, they were quite the rag-a-tag bunch in those times. But one of the things in the end times there, we had some bullies, eh. They kind of bullied us. We would gang up on them, so that it kind of stopped the bullying.

But I would say my best years were there. After I got out of the boarding school, I started to live at home. There were tougher years there. For myself, boarding schools were enjoyable to me.

9

Georgina Gregory

Despite the government's intention to civilize, educate, and assimilate the Indians, these personal accounts of residential school experiences reveal less than glowing accounts of life in the schools as experienced first-hand by the people who survived the experience. This final story from Georgina Gregory describes her experience at the File Hills Indian Residential School in Balcarres, Saskatchewan, that she believes severely traumatized her emotionally as well as psychologically. She documents the devastating lifelong damage she feels the residential school created for her. The story was told to Arlene Johnson.

One of the most traumatic experiences I have lived through was receiving an education "from the King." It all began a long time ago, but it has had far reaching effects, largely negative. The nightmares and bad dreams that I suffer frequently are caused directly from that process that was meant to educate and enlighten me. I also find that I still struggle with my identity as a human being, which is attributed to that same process.

I was seven years old when my parents took me to the boarding school I was to attend for the next eight years. I would have been there a year earlier but I had to wait for my younger sister to come also so that we would not be there alone.

The first thing that I remember was how it all smelled and looked. Those long and gloomy hallways and dark colours were most forbidding and intimidating. I had never seen anything like this before. There were other children being brought to the school for the first time that September day and others returning who had been there before. Most of the younger children were crying; others walked away quietly and thoughtfully after their parents left. We were all young, however, and we all began to play together. It wasn't too long before we learned that this was a place of learning. Yes, learning that white was right and that we and our parents were all wrong. I began to learn rather quickly that we had to obey and almost worship those white staff that were in charge of us. I remember one early experience I had that same fall. The children were all coming down with measles and the flu and so most of the windows were darkened in the dormitory and the beds were filled with sick children. I was one of them. I hadn't eaten for two days and I had a high fever. The matron forced me to eat but I vomited it out onto the floor. She order me out of bed and told me to clean it up. My head was spinning and my knees were shaking. I could hardly stand up but an older girl saw me and offered to clean up the mess. Other children suffered such treatment but it was all part of the learning process.

I remember seeing girls and boys strapped and beaten because they had taken some old crusts of bread to eat. The strapping alone was terrible but it seemed necessary to do it in front of the whole school looking on in fright. All of the students wondered who would be next and why.

I soon loved the classroom because it was away from the living area. Here we learned to sing songs about England and the King and far away places I had never heard of before. It was an escape, however, a kind of refuge. The smell of the new books and the pencil sharpeners were never threatening and the teacher seemed to appreciate the students' willingness to learn. Somehow the teachers in the classroom weren't as bad as those who supervised back at the residence.

There were children who would arrive now and then who could not speak English. They were ridiculed and discouraged from speaking their language and had no choice but to speak

English. Now I know there is absolutely nothing wrong about learning English, but they saw to it that those students forgot their language through humiliation and shame. Yes, there were things like "mouth exercises" in the classroom. I can't remember how many times I repeated along with everyone else, "Mr. Brown goes round the town" or "cold, old mouse in a house by the sea."

The boys and girls never mixed in boarding schools. There was always a side for the boys and a side for the girls in everything. We weren't allowed to speak at the table or to our brothers except on designated evenings for fifteen minutes. This was carefully supervised and someone from the staff would watch the clock to make sure you didn't go over your fifteen minutes. It was heart rendering to see a big brother and a little sister exchanging little gifts like a pencil and eraser in token of their feelings for each other because there wasn't anything else to give.

Most of the work done in the boarding school that I attended was done by the children. Yes, there was staff all right but they only supervised the operation after they had shown you how to do the job. Some children learned to work so well that they only worked and didn't attend classes. One very exciting time every month was when the supervisor would read out our new duties for the following month. Most students liked to work where there was food to handle because they might get an extra piece of bread if they didn't get caught. I remember seeing two boys carry out a large garbage can and watching the boys scramble for the scraps in it when they were out of sight of the ever-watchful eye of the person on duty.

At night after the supervisor had gone downstairs and the children were thought to be sleeping, visiting would start. We would talk softly of home, moms and dads, little sisters and little brothers. There would be those who cried quietly because they were lonely; others would be trying to comfort them. We all lived for the day when we would be going home for the summer. It seemed like it would never come; every so often someone would count the number of days left before the end of June. There would be excitement for awhile but seventy-five days is a long time for a child and soon the excitement wore off. We didn't get to see our parents very often after we were taken there. In my early years at the boarding school we were allowed to go home on New Years' Day and for the months of July and August. Our parents too were quite powerless in those times. They did not wish us to go to boarding school but they were threatened by the law if they didn't comply; we were all victims.

One of the hardest things to watch was the way we lived in total submission to those white staff members. We all sat down at meal times to our meagre meals while they sat out in front at another table and dined sumptuously. Indian girls with little white aprons and caps waited on them. A little bell would ring and the girls would get up to serve another cup of tea or a second helping. We could very well starve or go to bed if we complained.

It is no wonder that some of those folks look back with nostalgia to the "good old days." Yes, they really "had it made." I seem to recall that even their clothes were too good to be washed along with ours...of course, they weren't dirty Indians.

It seemed that it was customary to quarantine the school on an annual basis. Not necessarily because there was any illness around either. During those times from November to the end of March, no one could come to the school nor could any children go home. The staff continued to go to town every weekend. It was during one such time that another girl and I contacted some kind of eye infection. They treated us at the school with what they had but never tried to take us to a real doctor in town. This continued for at least three months; then the quarantine sign was removed and parents came to see their children immediately. My mother came too and was so enraged by what she had found that she took me home with her. My leaving didn't come about that easily however because she quarrelled with the principal, then later with the Indian Affairs agent. My parents then took me to see many eye doctors but it was too late. The one thing they all said was they might have been able to help if they had seen to me sooner. Today I have no eyesight. I wonder how many others in boarding schools have experienced similar problems. One boy died in school while I was there. My father talks about death and suicide during the time he was there.

They were determined to make ladies and gentlemen out of us and so we were taught how to talk, walk, and how to behave when there was white people around. What they refused to see was that Indian people always respected their elders. One of the methods employed was humiliation. If we did not obey at any given time we could be made an example of to ensure obedience from everyone. Indian people who are shy by nature would almost rather die than be slapped around publicly. It happened many times, however, and many former students from these schools still feel the shame and humiliation.

Why was it necessary to take away the Indian's language? Why was it necessary to make them ashamed of their culture? Why was it necessary to play God? The Indians knew another kind of God—a God who had fed them and had protected them for centuries...and now this.

We did learn to read and write and to do some math. Most of the texts gave the impression that Indians were wild and animal-like. It is no wonder that some children refused to learn. How could they identify with material like that? There are those who believe that Indian people are less intelligent than their white counterparts. If given the right atmosphere and material, Indians learn fast and as much as anyone else.

We didn't dare think about running away from school. I remember an episode when seven older girls made an attempt to escape. They were thrashed severely, had their hair all cut off, and had diarrhoea inflicted on them with an overdose of castor oil, then sent to bed for a week. If and when one child ever managed to reach home, the parents were so afraid that they saw to it that he or she returned because they too were told they would be punished and would go to prison if they didn't co-operate with the authorities. All Indian people were victims of the system.

There were many happy moments however, even though they were few and far between. The annual Halloween and Valentine's parties allowed us to get together with the boys and play games for a couple of hours. This was always well supervised of course. There was also the annual Christmas concert where everyone participated by singing, reading Bible stories, or acting out plays. Needless to say, we all knew our parts well.

Religion was a major part of life at the school. We had services twice on Sunday and various prayer meetings throughout the week. The main thrust of this was that God is love and that we needed to be saved because we were pagans. An old lady by the name of Mrs. Ribbons used to come and work around the school grounds. She was very old but she would gather leaves with her hands and put then in her apron, then haul them away to garbage cans. Not realizing she was working on Sunday and this was a Christian school, she came to work as usual. At dinnertime I remember the matron trying to shove Mrs. Ribbons through the door because she couldn't eat there that day. "You see, Mrs. Ribbons you don't work on Sundays and so can't feed you today," was what the matron said. The only wages Mrs. Ribbons ever got were the meals at the school.

Indian children in our school did not play Indian games. One spring evening there was some excitement on the boy's playground. Our windows were all painted so we girls were unable to see what was going on from the playroom. We all went outdoors to look. The boys were playing pow-wow, drumming on a pail. As a result they were all ordered indoors and sent to bed.

Everything that was done in the school was done in an army-like fashion. A bell rang—we all lined up; a whistle blew—we all came in for the evening duties; another kind of bell rang for meals—the children lined up again. We were so well-trained regimentally that we didn't have to think anymore.

It is very difficult to try and imagine what those in power felt Christianity really was. I am of the opinion that they didn't understand and used it as a tool or vehicle to serve their own interests—forget about loving thy neighbour.

I didn't know what hate, resentment, or rebellion were at that early age. They became a part of me later on. Today, I still have many lonely dreams and nightmares always involving the old boarding school. I cannot even visit the old site without having a pang of fear or some chill. I also still have the tendency to call every white person "Mr." or "Miss" depending upon who I am addressing. It took me years and years before I could admit I was an Indian even to myself. I suppose this was natural after being raised in an environment that held little or no respect for Indians.

Part III

*Pastahow**

*Cree word that used to mean "whatever you do now sets the pattern for the future." It has come to mean "sin."

10

Resistance

These stories provide some insight into the residential school experience that only the students who attended these schools can provide. The stories do not rely on any archival or government records, only the memories of those who tell them. But they are important because accounts derived from written sources cannot possibly present the entire residential school experience. As the stories of the negative experiences surface, there also needs to be acknowledgement of the acts of courage and resistance the children and parents adopted while living under the repressive policies of the Indian Act, which supported the residential school system. This chapter will look at these acts of courage and resistance.

To begin the healing process, stories about the emotional, physical, and sexual abuse need to be told, but there must also be a celebration of the stories of resistance. These stories are important, not only to former students, but also for those First Nations generations who came after the schools closed. It provides for us some reasons for the displacement that is found in our community.

I believe the resistance stories that have filtered through these interviews embody the spirit and courage of the children who attended these schools. The resistance was so constant that many of the acts were not even recognized by the interviewees themselves. If resistance as defined in the dictionary "is the act of resisting; or to resist as to oppose actively; strive against or to withstand" then the stories gathered for this project and other stories found elsewhere state one clear and emphatic message. There was resistance to the oppressive policies of the federal government regarding Indian residential schools.

One of these government policies included the dreaded "pass" system. This system was carried out as department policy despite the absence of legislation to effect enforcement. The pass system was introduced in 1885 as a result of the Riel uprisings.[1] Although Edgar Dewdney, Commissioner of Indian Affairs, recognized the lack of legislative power to enforce it, the pass system was in place for the next seventy years. Even after the 1951 revisions to the Indian Act repealed the Act's most repressive provisions, the policy was still used by some Department of Indian Affairs staff in certain parts of the country. An elder and former chief of a central Alberta band remembers asking permission of the staff from Indian Affairs to visit a doctor in Edmonton during the early 1960s. The pass system was also used at the residential schools to limit the number of visits children had with their parents. In some cases, the pass was only given to parents with strict instructions that they were not to interfere with their children's education or to try to bring them home.

Other policies that were used in tandem to promote the existence of the schools were withholding rations and deposing chiefs. The Indian agent could limit the amount of rations a family could receive if their children were not attending school, and chiefs were deposed if they refused to send their children to the schools. Chief Whitebear lost his government-recognized chieftainship for his reluctance to send his children to school. Chief Starblanket was allowed to reclaim his chieftainship if he would allow his children to be sent to residential school. These policies were combined with the provision for compulsory education to ensure the continuation of the residential school policy.

RESISTANCE TO GOVERNMENT POLICY

There are a few accounts or research studies published about the resistance of Canadian Indian people against federal Indian policy. Few Canadian or Indian studies texts present the stories of Indian resistance movements. Other than the military action at Batoche, the Frog Lake Rebellion, or Duck Lake, few accounts are reported, and there are even fewer accounts of non-violent Indian resistance movements.[2] Early Indian organizations are rarely mentioned, despite the fact that they initiated many changes in the living conditions of Indians across Canada. For example, in 1883 Chief O'Soup and other Treaty Four Chiefs from Saskatchewan's Qu'Appelle District travelled to Ottawa to protest the failure of the department to live up to treaty provisions.[3] In 1921, there were over fifteen hundred delegates at the League of Indian Nations Conference on the Samson Indian Reserve in Hobbema, Alberta.[4] Other resistance communications were made to Ottawa, including petitions, letters, and delegations from various chiefs across the country.

In my discussion with residential school survivors, including both family and friends, other stories of resistance surfaced. These stories included runaway boys trapping food to supplement their meagre meals and girls climbing out of third-storey windows to freedom. They were burning schools and defiantly challenging their oppressors. There were also the passive, subversive methods of resistance. In the early part of this century, a sign language developed that became a standardized method of communication for all schools across the country. The elements of these resistance stories are as poignant as any story of resistance by an oppressed people. What makes these stories and the people who lived them even more courageous was that these acts of resistance were carried out by children.

Parents and chiefs are included in this resistance movement. Chief Starblanket of the File Hills agency refused to send the children from his band to residential school. As a result, he was branded a troublemaker, and soon afterwards was deposed as chief by the Department on the charge that he had slaughtered an agency cow for his hungry band. Later, the Department offered to return his chieftainship if he allowed the children from his band to attend residential school. He eventually agreed in 1912, and his children were sent to the File Hills residential school.[5]

Later, after his children were taken to school, Chief Starblanket heard that the Governor General of Canada was to be travelling near his reserve. He made a formal request to meet with the Queen's representative, but was refused. As if he knew that he would not be able to meet with him, Chief Starblanket had prepared a written text for the Governor General. Later, it was found in archival records of the Department.[6] It read,

> In the treaty we made then, the government promised to
> make a school for every band of Indians on their own re-

serve, but instead, little children are torn from their mothers' arms or homes by the police or government agents, and taken sometimes hundreds of miles away to large schools, perhaps to take sick and die when their family can not see them. The little ants which live in the earth love their young ones, and wish to have them in their homes. Surely us red man are not smaller than those ants.

Other stories of resistance came from the children who attended the schools, including many stories of runaways. This seemed to be a common occurrence at the schools. Eleanor Brass tells of the runaway who was beaten to unconsciousness; Inez Deiter's interview talks about three runaway attempts, one of them being her own escape attempt. In her interview she talks about two couples who ran away where the students received the typical punishment for runaways. Inez recalled that their heads were shaved and their bodies beaten.

In the book, *John Tootoosis*, William Wuttunee said his younger brother was a runner.[7] Noel would be brought back and beaten in front of the school's residents. William and other family members would be forced to watch. William Wuttunee also remembers the number of runaways who died from exposure. Johnny Yesno, a Cree broadcaster and actor, remembered his runaway experience. He was eleven years old when he ran away. When he was caught, he was escorted back to the school by the RCMP on the train in handcuffs. The penalty for runaways was either a strapping, having your head shaved, or both. It was common practice to have the RCMP bring back runaways. Sheila Deiter remembers her father, Wilfred Deiter, talking about his experiences running away from File Hills. He said that after the RCMP had brought him back, they challenged the school administrator demanding to know why the children kept running away.

Another part of the resistance was the subversive methods used by the students to supplement their food source. All of the students except one spoke about their constant hunger while attending the schools. They tell that there simply was not enough food for growing bodies to eat. Ben Stonechild, one of the later students at File Hills, tells about young boys trapping small animals for food. Apparently, this practice was so well organized, that the young boys had pots and cooking utensils outside in the nearby bushes to cook their catches. The practice must have been well established as he mentions parents bringing bannock on visiting days to exchange for rabbits from the young boys. Inez Deiter mentions that stealing food from the kitchen was a constant occurrence. Bette Spence talks about the regular catches at the vegetable garden. Eleanor Brass wrote about stealing apples and being strapped on her back for it.

Interestingly enough, there seems to have been a high incidence of residential schools being burned. Inez Deiter mentions the burning of the Onion Lake School. She maintains it was a student at the school who set the fire. The first school at File Hills was also destroyed by fire. Former students state that this school fire was also set by students. John Tootoosis mentions the fire at the Delmas residential school in 1948 and, while there were no charges laid, the RCMP questioned the students asking who set the fire. Tootoosis maintains the fire was not set deliberately but that the old school was a fire hazard.

The disturbance in 1962 at the Edmonton Indian Residential School was more recent. From accounts by former students it appears "the riot," as it was called, started as a reaction to the practice of "icing."[8] Icing was used by the staff to punish children for some infraction of school rules. If a child broke a regulation, such as speaking their native language, the supervisor "iced" the wrongdoer. This meant that other children were not allowed to talk to this individual for a length of time. If another student spoke to the wrongdoer that person would be iced as well.

The Edmonton riot was the result of the frustration the children felt over this practice and other regulations laid down by the school administrators. Older students at the school blockaded the road into the school, and threw a burning mattress outside the window. These students were not passive about what they perceived to be injustice. The sixties had hit the residential schools.

While no doubt there were other forms of resistance used by the children, one of the most interesting was sign language. The language was developed in response to the need for children to communicate; not unlike the start of sign language for deaf children. For the children at the schools, not talking was the norm. The Victorian ideal "children are to be seen and not heard" was carried to the extreme. In addition, children were forbidden to speak their native language. As well, children from different tribal groups were often placed together, which discouraged use of a common native language. All of these reasons contributed to the start of some silent means of communication—a sign language.

There has not been anything written about this silent form of communication used at the schools. To my knowledge, this will be the first. I knew about the language as a young girl. My father and mother would use the sign language when they did not want my siblings and me to know what they were communicating. I forgot about their use of the language until many years later. My father had passed away, and my younger sister's daughter was diagnosed as profoundly deaf. I asked my mother if my niece could use the sign language that she and my father used when we were children. She said no, that that was the sign language they used at residential school.

As a student of anthropology at the University of Alberta, I found the sign language fascinating. First of all, it was children who devised a standardized sign language that was used across western Canada. I believe it was standardized in that my father and my mother understood each other. Yet my father was sixteen years older than my mother and had attended the File Hills residential school and the Birtle school in Brandon, while my mother attended the Roman Catholic schools and Anglican residential school at a much later date.

As well, this language was still considered to be subversive, or at least not important enough to be discussed by some former students. Still, I received confirmation of the language from several people. Bertha Buffalo of Hobbema showed me similar hand gestures for a sign language that was used at the Edmonton residential school. She also said the language was in use at the Hobbema residential school. Carl Urion said the language was used at Blue Quills residential school. Inez Deiter used the language at Onion Lake and St. Albans in Prince Albert; Walter Deiter at the File Hills, Brandon, and Birtle schools. Victor McNabb, a former student at the Gordon school remembers using the sign language while fishing outside the school. He said you couldn't yell across the lake but you could sign to make a message known.

Other students tell about using the two-handed form of communication behind a teacher's back in the classroom. Unknown to the teacher, students would be communicating and commenting during class. Inez Deiter said the language was used to convey birthday greetings to family members, since siblings were separated from each other and not allowed to talk to each other.

The sign language consisted of a two-handed letter system and body gestures. As an adult, Inez Deiter attended an American sign language course for her granddaughter. She showed the instructor the sign language she used at residential school. The instructor informed her that the language she used was the British form of signing. This particular form is no longer in use in the Americas, indicating that whoever introduced the sign language into the residential school did so before American sign language became the norm for the deaf community.

While there needs to be further research done on the introduction of this sign language, to me its very existence puts a new perspective on the residential school experience. The idea that these children, despite the hardships, found a means of communicating with one another is remarkable. The method in which the language was taught to newcomers is very much like any other language instruction. Inez Deiter said it took her a year to learn all the signs and gestures. The fact that this language endured over several generations is even more astounding and more language-like. Mel H. Buffalo attended the Edmonton residential school during the 1960s where he says the gestures were still in use—for example, a pulled ear meant a supervisor was coming.

These children were denied the basic right to speak, let alone the right to speak in their own language so they developed a language they could use. This language should be a testament to the intelligence, spirit, and resourcefulness of First Nations children.

11

The Effects of Residential Schools

Fear of caretakers, loneliness, knowing that elders and family were far away. Loathing from learning to hate oneself, because of the repeated physical, verbal or sexual abuse suffered at the hands of various adult caretakers. This is only a small part of the story.
Chief Ed Metawabin, Fort Albany First Nation, 1990[1]

Many First Nations people, and others, have blamed the high number of health and addiction disorders, the high suicide and overall mortality rates, the family and community disintegration on the effects of attending residential schools.[2] Some survivors and their communities have lost the skills needed to be healthy individuals. The loss of nurturing parents; loss of parenting skills; loss of identity; low self-esteem; the inability to think independently; the lack of unity within families and communities; the loss of language, culture, and respect for self; and finally, the loss of spiritual values have left communities in chaos.

Although there needs to be extensive research and analysis to evaluate the role of the residential school system in creating these social problems, connections already can be drawn between the behaviour and attitudes towards the children, and the effects of these behaviours on the children, and others, as adults. The primary goal of the schools was assimilation. Government and church officials wrote that the assimilation process would be successful if

Indian children were taught the white man's ways, away from the influences of their Indian parents and community.[3]

Issues surrounding the separation of parents from children over several generations have been a focal point of some discussion. In her article "The Effects of Residential Schools on Native Child-rearing Practices," N. Roslyn Ing identifies the breakdown of traditional and cultural child-rearing patterns as a major result of the schools. She also identifies the introduction of a European parenting style that was in direct opposition to the First Nations' attitudes towards children. Her argument is that the impact of the regimented European parenting style, based on corporal punishment, generated an intergenerational cycle of abuse within First Nations communities.[4]

I have already explained that the philosophy of Plains tribal groups toward children is based on love and tolerance, in contrast to the European model of parenting. The following is a list of attitudes towards children that would have been inculcated in Indian children through the schools' administrators. The list was developed and published by Alice Miller in *For Your Own Good*. Miller, a noted child psychologist, studied European child-rearing texts, mostly German, that were popular during the early part of this century. These attitudes include:

1. A feeling of duty produces love.
2. Hatred can be done away with by forbidding it.
3. Parents [*or any authority figure] deserve respect simply because they are parents.
4. Children are undeserving of respect simply because they are children.
5. Obedience makes a child strong.
6. A high degree of self-esteem is harmful.
7. A low degree of self-esteem makes a person altruistic.
8. Tenderness (doting) is harmful.
9. Responding to a child's needs is wrong.
10. Severity and coldness are good preparations for life.
11. A pretence of gratitude is better than honest gratitude.
12. The way you behave is more important than the way you are.
13. Neither parents [*nor authority figures] nor God would survive being offended.

---

*author's note

14. The body is something dirty and disgusting.
15. Strong feelings are harmful.
16. Parents [*or authority figures] are creatures free of drives or guilt.
17. Parents [*or authority figures] are always right.[5]

In addition, Miller wrote that adults were the masters of children, and that a child's will must be broken at all costs. She called this type of parenting "poisonous pedagogy." Miller connected Adolf Hitler's sadistic childhood at the hands of his father to the monster he would later become. She said that if children are raised with these attitudes, the state would produce citizens who are more likely to follow autocratic rulers. Some First Nations people claim that these values and attitudes are too prevalent within our community today. They argue that some form of autocratic leadership and autocratic parenting techniques have made for a further oppression of First Nations people.

Other issues connected with the loss of being parented have been catalogued. While not identified with First Nations residential schools, mainstream psychologists implicate the loss of parenting as the key cause for obsessive-compulsive disorders such as alcoholism, drug addiction, gambling, smoking, and overeating, to name a few. Psychologists Laurie and Jonathan Weiss bring transactional analysis expertise into a discussion of co-dependency. In *Recovery from Co-dependency* they say that

> We generally try to take care of ourselves and get our relational needs met in the same way we were parented, whether that parenting was functional or not. When it was dysfunctional, we try to anesthetize and repress the pain of our unmet early needs through various addictions and compulsions, and through co-dependent relationships.[6]

Co-dependency has been defined as a personality disorder caused by excessively rigid rules imposed in childhood and the loss of being parented in a loving and nurturing family home.[7] Children who attended residential school did not have the opportunity to live in a loving and nurturing home because of the provisions of the Indian Act that said Indian children must attend residential schools. The loss of being parented in a loving home leads, of course, to poor to non-existent parenting skills in the children who are now adults. If the condition is untreated, these losses are passed on to the next generation.

First Nations parenting skills were traditionally handed down through generations of experiential learning based on respect and nurturing. Traditional Plains tribal families rarely resorted to physical violence in order to teach a child. Children were highly regarded and respected, as were all the human creatures of the earth placed here by the Creator. The schools forcibly removed these children from the influence of their parents and community, and their gentle teaching. Once at school, the children were stripped of their personal possessions, identity, family, and tribal associations; given numbers and herded into dormitories where the dehumanizing process of assimilation began.

Stories of residential school survivors are filled with memories of neglect and violence. Other survivor stories can be found in any of the books mentioned in this text. The survivors painfully recall caretakers who were more concerned about rules or their own needs than those of the children.

A number of similarities regarding the practices of residential school staff members are recounted in this book and others. Most interesting is the lack of trust shown by administrators towards the children, and the effect it had on them. In Bette Spence's interview she tells of a school supervisor locking Betty and other girls in a room until one of them confessed to a theft that was later found to have been done by a non-Indian staff person. In this situation, after being locked up for some time, the girls were asking each other to confess to the theft, even when they knew they were innocent. Inez Deiter and Eleanor Brass both provide accounts of school administrators accusing the students of stealing apples. This lack of trust and other methods of denigrating the students—name-calling, subservience to staff needs, obedience—has had very negative results in our communities. We have lost the ability to believe in ourselves and other First Nations people.

Uniformity, perfectionism, and complete obedience were demanded of the children who attended these schools. Taught with severity, harsh discipline, and public humiliation, denied any exposure to their parents' nurturing parenting skills, denied any exposure to positive models for any type of relationships, how could these children possibly become loving parents themselves? Inez Deiter says of her experience, "To prepare us for life with our own families, we didn't know anything. We didn't know parenting skills."

The stories of the survivors show that the severe methods of corporal punishment, coercion, humiliation, and regimentation of children worked towards making them into obedient and silent victims. As one survivor, Georgina Gregory stated, "It wasn't too long before we learned that white was right and that we and our parents were all wrong. We had to obey and almost worship those white staff that were in charge of us."

Residential school took away their identity and self-esteem from many of the children. The erosion of their identity was accompanied by other methods of denigration such as name-calling or the vilification of culture and language. Three of the interviews mention that the children were not allowed to speak their Indian languages at the school. J. R. Miller discusses the vilification of a culture; in his book there is an illustration of a mural, made by the local school administrator, that shows Indians dressed in traditional outfits going to hell while white priests were on a staircase heading towards heaven.[8] These activities were supported by government policy that made it illegal for all Indian people to practise their traditional ceremonies.[9]

Public humiliation was the norm for children who were thought to be insubordinate. Eleanor Brass witnessed several beatings carried out in front of the children of the school. Inez Deiter tells of the children watching the administrators shave the heads of the runaways. Georgina Gregory talks about the humiliation the Indian children felt after they were slapped by school staff.

Even more troubling was the liberal use of corporal punishment against children. Every interview mentions a story of beatings that happened at the school. All of these tactics, methods, and policies led to an environment of denigration and degradation. However, the final devastation was the destruction of cultural and spiritual values. First Nations spirituality is based on respect, humility, sharing, and group harmony. These values were not honoured by the school administrators. Traditional teachings that would have taught these values were transmitted by parents and elders of the community. The children would have been taught to respect all humans and creatures; to be kind to people; to not swear, lie, or steal. Inez Deiter says that "in order to survive we had to resort to a lot of things that were not normal. I was becoming sneaky, lying in order to survive. We used to have to learn to steal and lie and be sneaky." They did this in order to eat. Another survivor recalls how he was sad that we were not well cared for, "that is what got in my way of trying to live a good life in a good way. No one taught us children how to behave to each other."

These many experiences continue to haunt our children. You can hear and feel the pain in this letter to the editor of a national aboriginal newspaper, *Alberta Native News*.[10] The letter appeared after the press release telling how much money was used to finance the Royal Commission on Aboriginal Peoples. The writer, David Neels, is a First Nations man from British Columbia.

> Oh, Canada, the painful legacy your residential schools have left my people, my children. They have left us scattered across our homeland, struggling to regain our sense of self. They have left our families broken; grandpas, grandmas, mothers, fathers, and children scattered like windblown flower petals in the fall. Generations of our people, raised in those cold dormitories, now struggle to raise their children. They lack the parenting skills they would have learned from their mothers and fathers at home. I weep, Oh Canada, when I think of the pain of my people, my children.
>
> Oh, Canada, what do I tell my young children? How can they understand the long reaching effects those misguided institutions have had on our family? How can they understand that this tragic disease is passed on from one generation to the next? How can they know the source of our people's loss of self-esteem, inability to trust, the anger, the alcoholism, and even the child abandonment? Tell me how to make them understand, Oh Canada.
>
> Oh Canada, it is hard to raise three young children as a single father. I remember when she phoned me from the doctor's office to share the joyful news of our twins growing in her womb. I was not told that day I would be raising them myself. Tell me what to say to my young children when they ask for their mother? Help them to understand her pain, her loss. Help them understand that their grandpa and grandma also lost a part of themselves in those schools

a long time ago. Help them to understand that even though they no longer see these relatives, they are still loved.

I want to love you, Oh Canada, but it is hard. You see there is a mass psychosis in this land that is so widespread it has come to be accepted as normal. A denial of history, that makes its victims wonder if it is only their delusion, it makes them want to forget, makes them want to drink, makes them want to leave their children, makes them...

Oh Canada, tell me who to blame? Is it the church, is it the government, is it the public apathy? Tell me how to help my children, how to help their mother's pain? Of course today you have supplied "resources" to help us, counselors, inquiries, white papers, policy papers, Royal Commissions. In the end, Oh Canada, your $58–million Royal Commission will not help my babies.

Afterword

The interviews recorded for this book did not address the issue of sexual assault that may or may not have taken place at any of the schools mentioned. Since the interviews were undertaken, for the most part, by family members or young university students, it would be unlikely that the issue would arise in this interview context. I believe for these interviews that it is important to read what it is they are not saying about the residential school experience. I will add that at the time of printing there were twenty-one civil suits filed at the Court of Queen's Bench in Regina for allegations of abuse occurring at the File Hills Indian Residential school.

Appendix A
Residential Schools Referred to in *From Our Mothers' Arms*

SASKATCHEWAN
Cypress Hills Indian Residential School
Delmas Indian Residential School
File Hills Indian Residential School (1889–1949)
Gordon Indian Residential School, Punichy
Lebret Industrial School
Lorlie Indian Residential School
Onion Lake Indian Residential School
Prince Albert Indian Residential School
Qu'Appelle Industrial School
Regina Industrial School (1890–1910)
Round Lake Indian Residential School (1886)

MANITOBA
Birtle Indian Residential School
Brandon Indian Residential School

PENNSYLVANIA
Carlisle Indian Residential School

Appendix B
What Is The Healing Fund?

The Healing Fund forms one part of The United Church of Canada's response to new directions in First Nations communities.*

After many years of facing despair and challenge, signs of new life and hope are emerging in many First Nations communities. In part, the new energy comes from facing the past. For many First Nations the experience of residential schools caused deep hurt. Now those wounds are healing and First Nations are asking the church to be part of the healing process.

One reason for church involvement grows from the church's role as servant of a healing, life-transforming God. As such, the church nurtures initiatives of healing. A second reason is that the church, as an agent of the federal government, was deeply involved in residential schools. As an institution the church was part of the process of pain; it is now called to be part of the process of healing.

Recognizing this, the August 1994 meeting of the General Council established a fund to help First Nations communities respond to some of the painful dimensions of the residential school experience. The fund's three-year goal of $1 million will be raised by voluntary contributions from church members and others who may wish to contribute.

Money will be distributed to First Nations communities according to criteria developed by The Healing Fund Council. The Council is composed of representatives from the All Native Circle Conference and the British Columbia Division of Native Ministries.

Projects receiving support will be Native community initiated, based, and supported.

WHY IS THE UNITED CHURCH OF CANADA INVOLVED IN ISSUES SURROUNDING RESIDENTIAL SCHOOLS?
The United Church of Canada was one of the churches that, on behalf of the federal government, administered the residential school

---

*adapted by UCPH from *Why the Healing Fund: The United Church Response* (Etobicoke: The United Church of Canada, Division of Mission in Canada, n.d.)

system. As awareness grows of the damaging role that residential schools played and continues to play in the lives of many Native individuals and communities, the church has a moral obligation and a spiritual theological imperative to be part of the healing of those wounds.

The abuse of Native children in church-run residential schools was a serious issue for the United Church and must be faced with honesty and openness, says the 1991 report of the *Moderator's Taskgroup on Residential Schools.*

Repentance and reconciliation involve action as well as words of apology.

With humility and a new understanding of mission as partnership, the church seeks new ways of being with First Nations that enrich the lives of both the church and First Nations.

Tbe 1986 Apology of The United Church of Canada to its First Nations congregations was a sign of repentance. We need to demonstrate as a church that we want to contribute to the healing in tangible ways. While the goal of The Healing Fund is to raise $1 million to enable First Nations peoples to carry out the healing, the education of United Church people about the history and present day realities of Aboriginal peoples will be a significant part of the process.

> I believe The Healing Fund will result in increased understanding and commitment by United Church people to address the many injustices that have been perpetrated against First Nations peoples over the centuries.[1]

WHY WAS THE UNITED CHURCH INVOLVED AT ALL?

The United Church's involvement in Indian residential schools did not develop in a vacuum. In part, the Indian work, as it was known, arose out of a desire to share the Good News of Jesus Christ and a deep sense of compassion and commitment to justice.

The church had long demonstrated its belief that education should be available to all children, regardless of class, gender, ethnic origin, or religion. For the predecessors of the United Church, access to education for children of low-income families was an important strategy in the struggle to secure greater justice and to subvert the privileges of established elites. The churches ran schools for girls and for the children of immigrants until the public education system replaced schools for the privileged.

As the traditional economies of Native nations came under heavy pressure, with the killing of the buffalo and the creation of reserves, many in the church felt the best way to assist First Nations was to provide means to educate the young in new economic systems and trade, hence industrial schools. The *Moderator's Taskgroup on Residential Schools* notes the residential schools were seen by the churches not only as a vehicle for converting Native people to the Christian faith, but also as a way of equipping the younger generation of Native people to survive in world where the old ways had either been destroyed of were considered unworkable or unworthy, or both.

The problem was that the church required Native people to repent of being Native people if they wished to follow the Christian way.[2]

A BRIEF HISTORY OF UNITED CHURCH
INVOLVEMENT IN RESIDENTIAL SCHOOLS

The United Church of Canada, through its predecessors, the Methodist and Presbyterian Churches, has a relationship with First Nations that extends back to the early seventeenth century, almost to the time of initial contact.

THE EARLY DAYS

In 1620, in New France, the Recollects instructed young Native children, but soon abandoned the project. Ten years later the Jesuits tried, but again the project failed because Natives continued to show little interest in European schooling.

Methodist contact with Aboriginal peoples in Upper and Lower Canada led to congregations being established in First Nations communities around Montreal and sporadically scattered throughout what is now Ontario. The Methodist mission relationship in the northwest began when British Methodists arrived in 1840 to serve as chaplains to the Hudson's Bay Company and as missionaries to the Indians, but spent the majority of their time with the latter. This was thirty-five years before white settlers began to flood the prairies.

Missionaries in this early period tended to adapt to their hosts' way of life rather than impose their own. Some missionaries and their families virtually lost their ability to speak English as they made their homes in Native communities. This interaction mutually benefited both parties.

EXPANDING WEST

About 1860, the British Methodist missionaries began returning to England and the Methodist Church of Upper Canada started its expansion westward. First Nations leadership within the church started to be displaced, and a more coercive approach replaced the dialogue between Native and non-Native. The advance of European settlement in the west provoked massive disruption of traditional Native ways.

Methodist churches became a key institution in many emerging settler villages and towns. Mission activity on the west coast led to Methodist churches being established in a number of Native villages on the coast and into the interior of Bntish Columbia. Schools attached to the missions were opening rapidly.

The nineteenth-century Presbyterian interaction with Aboriginal peoples was less extensive, focusing on people working in the near and far north, such as Hudson's Bay factors (administrators) who were generally Presbyterian. In the period just prior to union in 1925, the Presbyterians also saw their role as serving the newly established non-Native communities in the west and, to some extent, in the near north.

PARTNERSHIP WITH THE FEDERAL GOVERNMENT

Schooling formed a key element in the church's mission to the Indians. Most early missions had a day school and, in some cases, a small residential school as part of their outreach.

The federal government did not become involved until the turn of the century when treaties and statutes required the government to fund and set the general policy framework for residential schools. The British North America Act of 1867 saw "Her majesty agree to maintain a school in each reserve hereby made whenever the Indians of the reserve shall desire it." The churches—primarily the Roman Catholic, Anglican, Presbyterian, and United churches—became agents of the government in running the schools.

Initially, the federal government entered the residential school project with enthusiasm, seeing the schools as a way of accomplishing its general assimilationist policy towards Aboriginal peoples, which was explicit government policy into the 1950s. Quotes like the following from Duncan Campbell Scott, Deputy Superintendent-General for Indian Affairs (1913–32), are not atypical "Our objective is to continue until there is not a single Indian in Canada that has not been absorbed into the body politic."[3]

The government accepted responsibility for capital expenditures (facilities and equipment) and paid most of the staff salaries through per capita operating grants. However, as the system progressed and Natives proved remarkably resistant to assimilation, the government sought ways to fulfil legal obligations at minimal cost.

Early in the century controversy began. Continual complaints of underfunding by principals of the schools record their dissatisfaction with the federal government's lack of realistic financial support. Lack of funding undermined the time and educational resources required to provide an adequate education. Students were required to work in gardens, farming operations, laundry, and cooking to maintain operations.

While the federal government generally set policy, the church administration created the day-to-day atmosphere and activity in the schools. The churches recruited personnel and nominated the principals or administrators, who had to be approved by the federal government. Recruitment was difficult. Staff turnover rates were high, and many staff members were insufficiently qualified both in terms of their professional background as well as their understanding of Aboriginal history and culture.

The much-criticized practices of allowing students to return home only once a year (and sometimes not even then) and enforced English-language speaking were based on government policy. Not much early *official* evidence exists that the United Church disagreed with or lobbied against these policies, although the archival records indicate unsuccessful individual staff attempts to secure permission from the federal government to carry out instruction in Native languages. Recollections by former staff and written records also indicate that Native languages were taught with or without permission in some United Church–operated residential schools.

THE ROLE OF THE BOARD OF HOME MISSIONS AND THE WOMAN'S MISSIONARY SOCIETY

In the United Church, supervision of school operations was carried out by either the Board of Home Missions (or an earlier equivalent) or the Woman's Missionary Society, and archival records indicate that the national bodies responsible for the United Church residential schools knew something was wrong. Beginning in the late 1940s, church officials supported the movement toward the provision of day schools, at least at the elementary level, which would be accessible to all First Nations communities and cooperated energetically in the simultaneous move to close residential schools. In 1947 the Board of Home Missions presented a brief to a Joint Committee of the Senate and the House of Commons recommending that residential schools be reviewed and possibly replaced with day schools.

However, even those church officials who knew the system was flawed and who worked hard to make changes had no awareness of the devastating effects of residential schools as they are being named and understood today.

HOW MANY RESIDENTIAL SCHOOLS WAS THE UNITED CHURCH OF CANADA INVOLVED IN?

Provision of one sum proves difficult. Schools opened and closed and available church records are not necessarily comprehensive. Some schools were categorized as industrial schools by the Department of Indian and Northern Affairs (and its predecessors) and may not have been included in its data as residential schools. There was also no distinction made at the turn of the century between day schools and residential schools.

Given all these qualifications, we can say that United Church schools ranged in number from a maximum of 13 down to 6 schools in the 1950s. The maximum number of separate facilities operated by all denominations was 80. The schools were predominantly in western Canada, with only one school in Ontario into the 1930s. As might be expected, the schools tended to be in regions where mission activity and churches had been started, but there is no immediate correlation between a particular denominational school and given Aboriginal communities. Children from one community, or even one family, may have attended several different schools run by different denominations. By 1969 all The United Church of Canada–operated residential schools had been shut down.

One hundred and fifty thousand Native youth are estimated to have attended a residential school of some kind.

Notes

PREFACE AND ACKNOWLEDGEMENTS

1. The United Church of Canada, "Apology Statement to Native Congregations in The United Church of Canada," 31st General Council, August 15, 1986.
2. Marion Best, Moderator, Naramata, BC.
3. Stan McKay, former Moderator, after the 35th General Council Meeting of The United Church of Canada, August 19-28, 1994, Fergus, ON.

CHAPTER 1

1. H. B. Hawthorn, ed., *A Survey of Contemporary Indians of Canada: Economic, Political, Educational Needs and Policies* (The Hawthorn Report), 2 vols. (Ottawa: Indian Affairs Branch, 1966).
2. The Indian Act, R.S.C. 1985, c. I-6.
3. *W.R.B. v. Plint* (1998), 165 D.L.R. (4th) 352 (B.C. Supreme Court).
4. See Chapter 10 for a fuller discussion of the Edmonton riot.
5. E. Brian Titley, *A Narrow Vision: Duncan Campbell Scott and the Administration of Indian Affairs* (Vancouver: University of British Columbia Press, 1986).

   In 1987 I enrolled in an Indian education class taught by Brian Titley at the University of Alberta. In his class I questioned perceptions of a before and after picture of an Indian student that showed the student in full Indian regalia on his arrival at the school and the change in his appearance after a few months. Of course, I knew the stories of abuse and deprivation that had taken place at these schools and asked about the picture of the boy. I said I thought his cheeks looked fuller and he appeared chubbier in the picture of him in his Indian regalia. Mr.Titley's perception of the picture differed from mine.
6. Cecelia Haig-Brown, *Resistance and Renewal: Surviving the Indian Residential School* (Vancouver: Tillacum Library, 1988).
7. Assembly of First Nations, *Breaking the Silence:An Interpretive Study of Residential School Impact and Healing as Illustrated by the Stories of First Nations Individuals* (Ottawa: Assembly of First Nations, 1994).
8. Roman Catholic Bishop Hubert O'Connor was charged with rape and indecent assault following incidents in the mid-1960s during his tenure as principal of the St. Joseph's residential school outside Williams Lake in BC. The former bishop of Prince George was the

highest church official ever charged in Canada with sexual offences (*Canadian News Facts*, 1993, p. 4678; J. R. Miller, *Shingwauk's Vision: A History of the Residential Schools in Canada* [Toronto: University of Toronto Press, 1996], pp. 331–32).

9. Linda Bull, "Indian Residential Schools, The Native Perspective," Thesis, M. Ed., typescript photocopy (Ottawa: National Library of Canada, 1991).

10. Linda Jaine, ed., *Residential Schools: The Stolen Years* (Saskatoon: Extension Division Press, University of Saskatchewan, 1993).

11. Miller, *Shingwauk's Vision*.

12. Phil Fontaine, letter to the *Regina Leader-Post*, October 31, 1990.

13. Mel H. Buffalo, "A Legacy of Chaos," letter to *The Globe and Mail*, December 4, 1990.

14. It is now a matter of public record that the federal government has paid more than $20 million to Aboriginal students who were sexually abused at residential schools. The final tally could be in the hundreds of millions of dollars. Ottawa has already reached out-of-court settlements in almost 200 cases, but still faces over 1,600 claims. The bulk of the $20 million has gone to former students of the Gordon Indian Residential School (Janice Tibbetts, *National Post*, November 25, 1998, pp. A1, A2).

15. Stories of sexual abuse at the Mount Cashel Orphanage in Newfoundland began to emerge in the 1970s but were not formally investigated by police until 1989. During the early 1990s, several members of the Roman Catholic lay order of Christian Brothers and a neighbour were convicted on numerous counts of indecent assault and sexual assaults of young boys. A Royal Commission established to investigate the charges of abuse recommended that the boys receive compensation from the Newfoundland government.

16. Canada, *Looking Foward, Looking Back,* Report of the Royal Commission on Aboriginal Peoples (Ottawa, Ministry of Supply and Services, 1996).

CHAPTER 2

1. J. R. Miller, *Shingwauk's Vision: A History of Native Residential Schools* (Toronto: University of Toronto Press, 1996).

2. Linda Bull, "Indian Residential Schools, The Native Perspective," Thesis, M. Ed., typescript photocopy (Ottawa: National Library of Canada, 1991).

3. J. P. Donnelly and Reuben Goldthwaites, eds., *Jesuits: Letters from the Missions. The Jesuit Relations and Allied Documents, 1896–1901* (Chicago: Loyola University Press, 1967).

4. Bull, "Indian Residential Schools."

5. Bull, "Indian Residential Schools."

6. Canada, *Looking Forward, Looking Back,* Report of the Royal Commission on Aboriginal Peoples (Ottawa: Ministry of Supply and Services, 1996) 1:158; Miller, *Shingwauk's Vision,* p. 97.
7. Canada, *Looking Forward,* 1:267.
8. National Archives of Canada, RG10 Reel C-8134 Vol. 6001, file 1-1-1, Vol. 1. Memorandum from the Department Superintendent-General of Indian Affairs Frank Oliver to the Deputy General, October 3, 1904.
9. NAC RG10, Oct. 3, 1904.
10. Henry Hind Youle, *Narrative of the Canadian Red River Exploring Expeditions of 1857 and of the Assiniboine and Saskatchewan Exploring Expeditions of 1858* (Edmonton: Hurtig, 1971) 2:126.
11. Sarah Carter, *Lost Harvests: Prairie Indian Reserve Farmers and Government Policy* (Montreal and Kingston: McGill-Queen's University Press, 1990), p. 48. The Edward Abenakew papers can be found at the Saskatchewan Archives.
12. *Alberta History,* 27(2), 29 (Calgary: Historical Society of Alberta, 1979).
13. Eleanor Burke Leacock, *Myths of Male Dominance: Collected Articles on Women Cross-Culturally* (New York: Monthly Review Press, 1987), p. 47.
14. David G. Mandelbaum, *The Plains Cree: An Ethnographic, Historical and Comparative Study* (Saskatchewan: Canadian Plains Research Centre, University of Regina, 1979), pp. 143, 144.
15. Miller, *Shingwauk's Vision*; Eleanor Brass, *I Walk in Two Worlds.* (Alberta: Glenbow Museum, 1967).
16. Carter, *Lost Harvests,* p. 173.

CHAPTER 10

1. Sarah Carter, *Lost Harvests: Prairie Indian Reserve Farmers and Government Policy* (Montreal and Kingston: McGill-Queen's University Press, 1990), p. 48.
2. Duck Lake (March 26, 1885), the first battle of the North-West Rebellion, was a victory for Indian and Métis forces, which defeated the North-West Mounted Police and a band of citizen volunteers. It was followed on April 2 by the incident at Frog Lake when Cree Indians killed nine white men, and in May by the Battle of Batoche, where Métis rebels resisted government forces for three days (May 9–12) before being overrun (*The 1998 Canadian and World Encyclopedia* , CD-ROM [Toronto: McClelland & Stewart, 1998], under "North-West Rebellion").
3. Carter, *Lost Harvests.*
4. Jean Goodwill, *John Tootoosis, As told by Jean Goodwill and Norma Sluman* (Winnipeg: Pemmican Publications, 1984).

5. Carter, *Lost Harvests*; Miller, *Shingwauk's Vision*.
6. In Goodwill, *John Tootoosis*.
7. William Wuttunee, in Goodwill, *John Tootoosis*.
8. The details of this incident were supplied to me by Mel Buffalo who was a student at the Edmonton school when the riot took place.

CHAPTER 11

1. Chief Ed Metawabin, Fort Albany First Nation, in *Looking Forward, Looking Back*, Report of the Royal Commission on Aboriginal Peoples (Ottawa: Ministry of Supply and Services, 1996), p. 377.
2. Mel H. Buffalo, "A Legacy of Chaos," letter to *The Globe and Mail*, December 4, 1990.
3. J. R. Miller, *Shingwauk's Vision : A History of Native Residential Schools* (Toronto: University of Toronto Press, 1996), p. 41
4. N. Roslyn Ing, "The effects of residential schools on Native child-rearing practices," *Canadian Journal of Native Education* 1991: 18.
5. Alice Miller, *For Your Own Good* (New York: Farrar, Strauss, & Giroux, 1983), pp. 59-60. The phrase "or authority figures" was added by the author.
6. Laurie Weiss and Jonathan Weiss, *Recovery from Co-Dependency* (Deerfield Beach, FL: Health Communications, Inc., 1989).
7. Weiss, *Recovery*, p. 13
8. Miller, *Shingwauk's Vision*, p. 192
9. Miller, *Shingwauk's Vision*, p. 205
10. April 1997.

APPENDIX B

1. Marion Best, Moderator, Naramata, BC.
2. *Moderator's Taskgroup on Residential Schools,* reported to the Sub-Executive of General Council, The United Church of Canada, Nov. 1991.
3. Quote from The United Church of Canada, "Why the Healing Fund: The United Church Response" (Etobicoke, ON: The United Church of Canada, Division of Mission in Canada, n.d.) Original source unknown.

Bibliography

Abenakew, Edward. 1973. *Voices of the Plains Cree*. Toronto: McClelland & Stewart.

Assembly of First Nations. 1994. *Breaking the Silence: An Interpretive Study of Residential School Impact and Healing as Illustrated by the Stories of First Nations Individuals*. Ottawa: First Nations Health Commission.

Best, Marion, Moderator of the United Church of Canada. Naramata, BC.

Brass, Eleanor. 1967. *I Walk in Two Worlds*. Calgary: Glenbow Museum.

Buffalo, Mel H. 1990. "A Legacy of Chaos." Letter to *The Globe and Mail*, December 4.

Canada. 1867. British North America Act. sec. 92 (24).

———. 1985. Indian Act, R.S.C., c. I-6.

———. 1996. *Looking Forward, Looking Back*, Report of the Royal Commission on Aboriginal Peoples. Ottawa: Ministry of Supply and Services.

———. 1904. National Archives of Canada, RG10 Reel C-8134 Vol. 6601. file 1-1, Vol. 1. Memorandum for the Deputy General of Indian Affairs. 3 Oct.

Canadian News Facts. 1991. Vol. 25, No. 8, April 16–30, p. 4366-3, "Natives Offered Royal Commission."

———. 1991. Vol. 25, No. 13, June 16–30, p. 4398-2, "Action Sought on Native Abuse."

———. 1992. April 16–April 30.

———. 1992. Vol. 26, No. 23, Dec. 16–31, p. 4678-2, Names in the News.

Canadian and World Encyclopedia, The. 1998. CD-ROM. Toronto: McClelland & Stewart.

Carter, Sarah. 1990. *Lost Harvests: Prairie Indian Reserve Farmers and Government Policy*. Montreal and Kingston: McGill-Queen's University Press.

Chrisjohn, Roland, and Sherri Young. 1997. *The Circle Game: Shadows and Substance in the Indian Residential School Experience in Canada*. With contributions by Michael Maraun. Penticton, B.C.: Theytus Books.

Donnelly, J. P., and Reuben Goldthwaites, eds. 1967. *Jesuits. Letters from the Missions. The Jesuit Relations and Allied Documents, 1896–1901*. Chicago: Loyola University Press.

Goodwill, Jean. 1984. *John Tootoosis, As Told by Jean Goodwill and Norma Sluman.* Winnipeg: Pemmican Publications.

Haig-Brown, Cecelia. 1988. *Resistance and Renewal: Surviving the Indian Residential School* Vancouver: Tillacum Library.

Hawthorn, H. B., ed. 1966. *A Survey of Contemporary Indians of Canada: Economic, Political, Educational Needs and Policies (The Hawthorn Report),* 2 vols. Ottawa: Indian Affairs Branch.

Hind, Henry Youle. 1971. *Narrative of the Canadian Red River Exploring Expeditions of 1857 and of the Assiniboine and Saskatchewan Exploring Expeditions of 1858,* vol. 2, p. 126. Edmonton: Hurtig.

Historical Society of Alberta. 1979. *Alberta History,* vol. 27 (2), 29.

Ing, N. Roslyn. 1991. "The Effects of Residential Schools on Native Child-rearing Practices." *Canadian Journal of Native Education* (18).

Jaine, Linda, ed. 1993. *Residential Schools: The Stolen Years.* Saskatoon: Extension Division Press, University of Saskatchewan.

Leacock, Eleanor Burke. 1987. *Myths of Male Dominance: Collected Articles on Women Cross-Culturally.* New York: Monthly Review Press.

Mandelbaum, David G. 1979. *The Plains Cree: An Ethnographic, Historical and Comparative Study.* Saskatchewan: Canadian Plains Research Centre, University of Regina.

McKay, Stan. 1994. After the 35th General Council Meeting of The United Church of Canada, at Fergus, ON, 19–28 August.

Miller, Alice. 1983. *For Your Own Good.* New York: Farrar, Strauss, & Giroux, 1983.

Miller, J. R. 1996. *Shingwauk's Vision.* Toronto: University of Toronto Press.

National Archives of Canada, *see* Canada.

Neels, David. 1997. Letter to *Alberta Native News.* April.

Tibbetts, Janice. 1998. *National Post.* November 25.

Titley, E. Brian. 1986. *A Narrow Vision: Duncan Campbell Scott and the Administration of Indian Affairs.* Vancouver: University of British Columbia Press.

United Church of Canada, The. n.d. "Why the Healing Fund: The United Church Response." Etobicoke: The United Church of Canada, Division of Mission in Canada.

——. 1986. "Apology Statement to Native Congregations in The United Church of Canada." 31st General Council. August 15.

——. 1991. *Taskgroup on Residential Schools.* Report to Sub-Executive of General Council, November.

Weiss, Laurie, and Jonathan Weiss. 1989. *Recovery from Co-Dependency.* Deerfield Beach, FL: Health Communications, Inc.

Photo Credits

page 6: Thomas Moore before and after attending the Regina Industrial School, n.d. Saskatchewan Archives Board, #R-A8223, 1 and 2.

pages 12 and 22: Fred Dieter at the Regina Industrial School, Walter Deiter and Eleanor Brass at the Brandon Indian Residential School, and Mary Wuttunee, Inez Deiter, Loray Wuttunee courtesy of the author.

page 17: Fred Dieter, left, and his barn, horses, and non-Native hired man, 1915. National Archives of Canada, John Boyd Collection, C-67099.